Contents

Preface

"Mr. Brown," he said, "we have a bell, and we ring it every Sunday morning. People know that we are here, and if they want to come to church they will."

That was the approach to communications of a senior officer in a congregation I once served. It may be a parable of the way the church has sometimes thought about communications: "We have it. Let them come and get it if they want it."

In the rest of our life, we operate with other presuppositions. If we look squarely at the church's mandate, we find an outward-moving dynamic which has had its most striking and comprehensive manifestation in missionary expansion. At its best, the dynamic has been seen and understood as much more than verbal; it has been primarily concerned with relationships, as Jesus put it in his statement of the Great Commandment, to love God supremely and to love our neighbor as ourselves.

Whatever else we may do or seem to do, we are primarily concerned with seeing the church effectively communicating God's love, forgiveness, and energizing power. Where we can do it better, we want to do so. It is for that purpose that these pages have been written.

Most of my experience has been in the area of the print medium. Since the design of this small book includes a few section headings involving other media, it will be recognized that my cursory references to them are advanced only in a spirit of sharing what I have learned or been told by others. Since most of my life has been spent in trying to report fairly and accurately what people are saying and doing, I can only hope that I have been fair to them and to the readers in this modest effort.

Aubrey N. Brown, Jr.

Introduction

A STANDARD OF EXCELLENCE

By nature the church is involved in communication. That communication is in many forms, but is chiefly verbal and visual. In its earliest form of communication, although the spoken word was central, there was a heavy emphasis on the visual, with signs and symbols. Later, works of art were used to tell the never-ending story of God with us, God's call to us, and God's claim on us.

The basic question is not whether to communicate. It is how and how well we are to do it. My conviction is that we are under a mandate to make communication, like anything else related to the church, the best possible. From the earliest Old Testament specifications for sacrifices, the "first fruits"—the best—were to be brought to the altar; what was offered to the Lord was to be "without spot or blemish."

While good stewardship will keep us from waste and extravagance, what we offer in the service of the church should meet the test of quality. How we maintain a church building communicates a great deal. How we plan and print a bulletin or newsletter, or how well we produce and project a set of slides or a filmstrip may tell even more.

To a considerable degree, the excellence or effectiveness of our own communication can have much to do with what others think of the validity of the claims of Jesus Christ and his kingdom. That claim, I think, calls for our best.

EFFECTIVE PROMOTION IS ESSENTIAL

Good planning and preparation for significant church events are not enough. I have seen too many well planned and practiced—and presented—events with only a handful of people who came to see them. A few posters in store windows or on bulletin boards won't do. Neither will a general notice in a newspaper. There are enough good ways, however, to exhaust our energies.

We know how we and others respond to one-to-one invitations and opportunities. We know how to use the telephone. For all kinds of personal, school, and community events, we share and get caught up in a contagion of enthusiasm and support. We know that when something is expected of us personally, we are more likely to meet that expectation than if an invitation is extended generally and to "everybody." A personal letter gets our attention (and response), whereas a

printed notice for the whole community may fail. If we are invited to help, and if we feel needed, we will be more likely to respond. There are innumerable ways to involve (not simply manipulate) people for constructive and mutually satisfying undertakings.

Sunday school classes can dry up on the vine because principles like these are not recognized as good and effective ways to share much that is constructive and interesting in such classes. In order to communicate effectively in these circumstances, we must recognize the importance of personal dignity, self-esteem, individual worth, and the need to be needed. When we do so, everybody will benefit.

THERE ARE COSTS

Good communication is costly, mostly in time and personal energy. In the context and outreach of a church, there is also a significant dollar cost. This is why our generous giving—remember that Old Testament phrase about the "first fruits," the best—makes possible what is needed.

WHAT A COMMUNITY SEES

Is there any better way a church proclaims its faith and commitment to a community more than in the way its people provide money for its life and mission? A church's physical plant, its ministry to the neighborhood and community, its response to physical and emergency needs—all of these give visible proof of a people's dedication, or lack of it.

Everything God wants us to do in and through the church and its outreach can be easily cared for with our gifts, not by our money-making efforts to extract cash from somebody else. It is our commitment, our obligation, our opportunity, and our giving that are blessed and multiplied by God.

Do we want our church to be known as the one with the best rummage sales and bazaars, or the one with a ready response of compassionate outpouring of generous provisions and service to street people or troubled neighborhoods?

What could do more to touch an indifferent and sometimes hard and cruel world than the sight or knowledge of an outpouring of concern and support to meet human need and suffering? I believe it is that image of the church that we deeply want and should seek and pray to become.

THE CHURCH'S EQUIPMENT

A church office should have the best equipment it is possible to provide. When publications go out with faint or smudged print on cheap paper, letterheads, and envelopes, something less than good is communicated.

Equipment can be purchased and depreciated instead of overwhelming a one-year budget. An accountant in the congregation can set up the depreciation schedule. Make-do, wait-a-while tactics are demoralizing. There must be good judgment and sensible economy, but borrowing is an acceptable business practice of securing funds for equipment needed in the church as well as elsewhere.

Good—or well-reconditioned—typewriters, duplicators, cutting boards, paper folders, postage meters, light boards, addressing equipment, word processors, whatever is needed for a first-class and creditable job should be purchased. The major cost in a church office is for labor. Whatever will make the labor more efficient and productive should be provided without hesitation. Not to do so is an incredibly poor business practice.

I am not suggesting that small churches, or those with small resources, mortgage their future away in unpayable equipment bills. I am urging that they do the best they can, including exploring the availability of rebuilt and reconditioned equipment.

How to Get It Done

Organization and Finance

Let's appoint a committee! When we confront any task or consider a new venture, out of experience or desperation, that is what we usually shout.

I have a feeling that the worst thing I could do is to encourage you to begin to deal with communication, or public relations, in your church in a comprehensive way by appointing a committee.

Many printed items come to me from churches, and I am able to keep in touch with the way a number of churches are organized. I could not name one church with a public relations or communications committee. Nor do I know of one with a budget for communications or public relations as such. True, most, if not all, of these churches could do more in this area than they are now doing, but I am not sure the lack is to be found in not having an overall committee.

My advice to a church is to start where you are with what you have. You may have one or more of these: a newsletter, a bulletin, occasional direct mail in the form of letters, perhaps a weekly advertisement in the newspaper. The newsletter may be handled by an editor, possibly with a committee or one or two others with special responsibility. All the rest are probably in the hands of a church secretary.

Your official board, or one of its committees, may have the general responsibility for the newsletter and for newspaper advertising. Within that framework, steps might well be taken to expand communications/PR responsibilities. But if you do not have, or cannot find, someone with some kind of demonstrated experience or interest, you may do well to wait.

You can do one thing, however, that can help. You can use an interest- or skills-finder to discover your available resources. My guess is that even in the smallest congregation you will find one or more persons whose daily work or past experience is in this field. Anyone who sells, for instance, has to be aware of and use the basic principles.

In addition to sales people, there are those with skills or responsibilities in public relations, communications, advertising, editing, writing, printing, paper supply, journalism, commercial art, photography, radio/TV, film-making, audio-visuals, tape and video recording, company publications, quick printing, typing, computer or word processor operations—the possibilities are vast in any community.

Full information about people with these and other abilities as they become members should be kept in a card file; better, information can be stored on a computer for quick retrieval. Then you know where to start in meeting specific needs. (After members are received into a church, it is good to give them a personally conducted tour of the entire church, showing them how and where everything is done. You never know what interests will be sparked or what sources of help will be discovered.)

My recommendation is to name task forces for specific jobs for the life of the job rather than naming a group of people with specific, but limited, talents to an overall committee to direct a total program. This method will not upset any already-established domains.

A well-selected task force to handle the promotion of a special event is more likely to do a better job than a committee with a whole bag of responsibilities. For

some ventures, like a centennial anniversary celebration, all task forces could be combined.

In due time, individuals will emerge from the specific assignments who might well seek to coordinate all aspects of a PR program, though I would not worry if this did not occur.

Financing the program can be handled in much the same way. The cost of the newsletter, the bulletin, and direct mail is probably already covered in one item related to office expenses or printing. Another item may be reserved for advertising. Let them stand. For other task forces or new ventures, look for something in contingency funds or in a special designation by the official board to care for it. If the venture proves to be valuable, then it might go into next year's budget. Moving in this way will forestall opposition to what may be considered too large an amount for an unproven enterprise. As new enterprises are given opportunities to prove their worth, different financial provisions may be combined with little or no opposition.

By taking a little more time, we are often able to achieve more than will a frontal attack and a demand for immediate approval of an ambitious new program.

Some church officers and leaders have no hesitation in providing whatever is needed to develop a good image of their business enterprise. When it comes to spending money in the area of publicity and communications for the church, they have some reservations. I, too, want to see churches use well the gifts that the people have given for Kingdom purposes. Moving into such a program in phases should give assurances of good intentions and astuteness.

The question is not whether we can afford it. It is, rather, with our recognized responsibilities and Christian commitment, can we afford not to do it?

Now keeping in mind our concern for a standard of excellence in what the church attempts to do, remembering that good planning and preparation also need good promotion, and with a commitment to providing the tools and equipment to get the job done, let us look at some of the opportunities that are ours in communication within the church and as we reach out into the community.

PART I

Strengthening Communication Within Your Congregation

Using the Printed Word

THE SUNDAY BULLETIN

Church newsletters may appear monthly, quarterly, or occasionally, but the bulletin for worship has to be produced, without fail, week after week, year after year. With its captive audience, it is undoubtedly the most thoroughly read printed work in a church.

What I have emphasized about the quality of printing, readability and good paper applies in full measure to the bulletin. Smudged or faintly printed sheets, crowded pages, errors in spelling or grammar tell something about a church that is unworthy. A clean, well-spaced, sharply typed and printed bulletin helps create confidence in the mission and leadership of the church.

For your church to have a commercially printed bulletin may be well worth the cost, but with the proliferation of efficient duplicating processes, more and more printed matter is being produced in church offices. If the type style is good and the printing is sharp, with strong contrasts, church office printing can be done with considerable savings. Also, if done in the church office, your bulletin can be printed on Friday, instead of having to meet a Monday or Tuesday deadline at a commercial printer, thus making possible the inclusion of last-minute announcements.

Bulletin covers should be well designed, and not always the same. Someone is available in almost every church or community to help with such a design. The same picture or drawing of a church building week after week becomes monotonous. If your printing process reproduces photographs well, and if you have access to good, interesting black-and-white pictures with sharp contrasts, your bulletin cover can be made exceptionally attractive. Pictures should be close-ups, not distant scenes of people, and cropped so as to eliminate distractions.

Colored ink, unless it is practically black, will not reproduce pictures well. Colored paper can be used to advantage only if it is a light rather than a dark color. It is disheartening to plan and type good material for a bulletin only to have it printed in such a way as to make it hard to read. Black ink on white paper, remember, provides the sharpest contrast.

Stock bulletins, with pages one and four pre-printed, may be useful in some churches. These are provided at a fairly nominal cost by some denominational national headquarters. With a churchwide or seasonal message on page four, a church's own material is printed on pages two and three.

Other stock bulletins, designed for special seasons like Christmas and Easter, or for other general uses, are available from church supply houses.

In planning how the information is placed on each page—the layout—it is important to remember that a generous use of white space makes printed matter stand out. Some routine announcements can be printed in two columns and in slightly smaller type than the rest of the bulletin.

Three principal purposes are served by the Sunday bulletin.

Directions for Worship. This is the central purpose, with the listing of hymns, scripture selections, prayers, responses and unison readings, music titles and texts, leaders of the service, greeters for the day, and others whose contribution should be recognized.

Procedures are also explained. These usually include type symbols showing when the congregation is to stand.

It is helpful when the text of the offertory anthem, or other choral works, is printed in the bulletin for all to follow. Here, a smaller type can be used to advantage, like so:

★ Offertory Anthem: Be Thou Exalted, Lord My God
Heinrich Schütz

Lord my God, be Thou exalted, and be Thou lifted up,
mighty art Thou, and Thou shalt reign forever, God eternal.

In printing directions to guide worshipers, it may be helpful to consider the fact that anyone dropping into one of our weekly services who has little or no "church" background would be confused and bewildered by some of the listings in the order of service that we take for granted. Although many long-time worshipers have seen and used the words for a lifetime, some people may not know what they mean. An occasional line or two giving background information on words like *invocation, doxology, choral introit, Gloria Patri, benediction,* and *postlude* would be of help to many and of interest to all. Perhaps even background information on words like *pulpit, sermon, hymn, baptism,* the different words used for the Lord's Supper, and even words like *church* and *congregation* may be explained.

Symbols in the church need frequent and repeated explanation and interpretation, along with architectural terms and features. Whatever a church building has—inside and out—from the rich history of Christian art and architecture needs repeated explanation and interpretation, from the design of the sanctuary and steeple to the words and symbols inscribed on the offering plates and communion table.

The traditional seasons and days of the Christian calendar deserve clear explanation and comment.

In these ways, and others, a bulletin can be an effective teaching aid.

Announcements of Coming Events. A church's regular (or changing) schedule needs to be emphasized in the bulletin listings. Events of the coming week deserve adequate attention. If there are many events, they may be arranged in two columns for easier reference. In some cases where copying machines can reduce the type size slightly, the listings may well be reduced.

If a person, especially an invited guest, is asked to speak or participate in a scheduled meeting, it is a courtesy to list that person's name and a bit of his or her background ahead of time.

A policy should probably be established to govern the inclusion of announcements of events that may not be directly or closely related to the work and interests of the church, even though church members are involved in them. Such announcements may be more suitable for the local newspaper.

Every bulletin should show the date, the full name and address of the church (if an intersection is shown, also give the street number on the principal street), names of church staff, office hours and telephone number. If it is not apparent from the name of the church, the denominational name should be indicated. Since a bulletin may wind up one or two thousand miles from its point of origin, the name of the town or city should always appear.

Education for Mission and Service. For the captive readership of a Sunday bulletin, with the reasonable assurance that what is in it will be read, few if any educational and informational avenues in a church offer a greater opportunity than this one. This does not mean that the bulletin should be a glorified bulletin board.

In the bulletin, brief glimpses into the worldwide activities being supported by the church can be capsulized, beginning with agencies and institutions in the community. Those who are volunteering their services in community enterprises deserve recognition and support. Area and community needs should be spelled out.

Special and seasonal offerings can be given appropriate emphasis in the bulletin, showing needs to be met and how and when offerings will be received. A follow-up in later weeks should always show how much was given. (The emphasis should be not simply on making a worthy gift, but also on increasing the knowledge of the givers in a phase of the church's on-going mission and service.)

This kind of education can also be carried on effectively in other ways in the bulletin. Information and opinions are available through denominational and other periodicals (sometimes the daily paper), from missionary letters, from annual reports and yearbooks, from prayer guides and calendars, and from travels and experiences of members of the congregation.

If all of these fail, almost every church has, or should have, a book of quotations of interesting and significant leaders and thinkers on almost any aspect of church service and involvement.

A close tie should be maintained with the church's library so as to have information about new books as they become available, or an occasional quotation from one of them as supplied by the librarian. A pastor's study or church library has collections of memorable quotations about missions, stewardship, prayer—the list is endless. Keep a file of items of different lengths that can be used to add information and interest to your bulletins.

It is a poor use of available space to print the list of church officers and heads of organizations each week or even once a month. Church members do need to have this list before them more than once a year. Printing the list in alternate months might be an appropriate schedule.

Ideas for Bulletin Fillers

★ Meaning of Christian symbols

★ Explanations of different parts of the worship service

★ Update on mission activities

★ Notices of special community needs

★ Inspirational quotations

★ Prayers

★ History of a hymn

★ Meaning of current Christian church season

Sermon Titles Communicate Something

I have no objection to listing sermon titles in the order of worship, on outdoor bulletin boards, or in newspaper advertising, if they are good. I regret to say that I rarely see good ones. I have a feeling that titling their sermons may be what preachers do least well of anything, and I have reason to believe that they may never have thought much about it.

Suppose the eye of a person who is indifferent to or alienated from the church falls upon a newspaper advertisement listing a sermon title. The reader says, "Let me see what the church is doing or thinks to be important these days." There it is in black and white for the major focus for the week: "The Bias of Baptism," or "Covered or Uncovered." This will only reinforce the reader's negative attitudes. In this way, sermon titles can be a stumbling block to evangelism.

A good title might stimulate interest in the minds of those who are planning to be present and cause them to do some advance reading. Look briefly at an assortment of sermon titles gleaned from the newspaper advertisements: What Is Faith? . . . The Messiah Revealed . . . Jesus' First Sermon in Nazareth . . . John the Messenger . . . David and Goliath . . . An Effec-

tive Church . . . In Communion with God . . . Heavenly Voice—Worldly Implications . . . Three Basic Needs . . . God's Story for Us . . . The Lord Hurts . . . Strength for the Journey . . . Sometimes It's That Way . . . Who Can This Be?

Which one of these would make you want to be present to hear what was to be said? Which one would tell unchurched or indifferent readers that preachers and churches are coming to grips with issues that matter?

Based on this kind of observation, I am inclined to believe that published titles usually miss the mark and may do more harm than good. Those churches whose tradition keeps them from announcing sermon titles would seem to be justified.

It is good and legitimate to announce a title if we can do it well. How much time and energy to give it is another question.

Now, which of the following do you think would interest you? On Finding It Hard to Believe in God . . . There Is No Death . . . When God Lets Us Down . . . On Being Fit to Live With . . . The Difficulty of Forgiving Our Enemies . . . The Towering Question—Is Christianity Possible? . . . The Constructive Use of Fear. . . On Worshiping Things We Manufacture . . . Six Ways to Tell Right from Wrong . . . Facing the Challenge of Change. All of these came from the mind of a master preacher, Harry Emerson Fosdick. He learned how to do it and so can we.

The Sermon Is By. . .

With the listing of the sermon title, the sermon is by—whom? How do you do it? The way in which a minister wants to be addressed, what he or she wants to be called, communicates something about the person and about the church's best recognized leader.

The New Testament makes it quite clear that the desire for status, for elevated positions, and for deferential preference in the marketplace are foreign to the spirit of servanthood, which should be the mark of a minister.

For this reason, I have had a running battle (a losing one) with any use of the honorific adjective *Reverend*, which is not a title and describes no function. My solution to the problem is to call the minister what most of the members of the congregation are called: Mr., Miss, Ms., or Mrs; with an earned doctorate, Dr. is appropriate. The sermon is by—Mr. (or Mrs. or Ms.) Doe. Or by "The Minister," or "The Pastor."

Mailing the Bulletin

Bulletins are mailed appropriately to shut-ins and other individuals who cannot attend church regularly or who miss a special service. (A personal written word on the bulletin helps.) Where a church's services are broadcast, it is customary to mail the bulletin ahead of time for use on Sunday.

In some cases, the bulletin and the newsletter are combined and mailed under second- or third-class permits. If this is done under second-class regulations, the nature of a portion of the contents must be modified. The post office will provide the particulars of this requirement.

All churches should bind their bulletins annually or biennially for preservation for historical or reference purposes. These volumes should be kept in the church library or in some safe place where single copies will not be removed or defaced.

NEWSLETTERS

Almost any church big enough to be a church should have a newsletter. It may well be the most important printed item in the life of the church.

Newsletters come in many sizes and descriptions; some are carefully and tastefully produced, others are poorly planned (or thrown together) and printed, reflecting small credit on the church or the claims of its mission.

Like everything else we do in the church, the newsletter deserves the best we can give it. This does not mean that it must be "arty" or extravagantly produced. It means that it must be well planned, using an appropriate type size and style, with suitable paper to produce a sheet that reaches out and holds our attention with contents so interesting that we can't help reading it.

What to Put in It

I take back nothing of what I have said in the last paragraph when I stress the fact that more important than anything about a newsletter's looks is what goes into it. Amazingly disorganized and poorly printed sheets are read with great eagerness if they are filled with interesting items and lively ideas with a big focus on people. They would be read much better if they met the specifications for a sheet that is also attractive.

One of the special advantages of a church newsletter is your opportunity to pay detailed attention to people in your church (and community) and to what they are thinking and doing. Therefore, don't let the newsletter become simply a promotional sheet for coming events, no matter how important these are. I have discussed elsewhere in these pages my deep concern that churches use all available good means to get their people to respond to planned programs and events. I do not minimize that, but the newsletter must be more than a promotional organ.

A newsletter should not carry the minutes of any

meeting. That would be deadly. The newsletter's purpose is to put a heavy emphasis on the people of the church, to build understanding and acquaintance among them, and to be a true means of communication.

There need never be a lack of material—good material—for the newsletter's columns as long as a church exists, because a church consists of people who are engaged in an infinite variety of enterprises. They have many different views on all kinds of subjects. Furthermore, the church is engaged in a worldwide, on-going mission carried out by the most interesting people you will ever know. You could never exhaust the possibilities in reporting their work and experiences.

There are numerous **sources of information** for the newsletter: the pastor, staff and officers, heads of committees and church organizations, church school officers and teachers, leaders of the music program, special committees and task forces, youth representatives and leaders, community agencies and institutions with which the church cooperates, regional and national denominational executives and publications, and what can be learned and used from other churches' newsletters. (Churches do well to exchange newsletters with a half-dozen or more congregations similarly situated.)

Many newsletters feature a **message from the pastor.** To keep this feature from becoming routine or one to be skipped over, the writers will want to consider reporting developments in the life and mission of the church, issues of concern in the community or denomination, needs or developments in a new congregational program, or commendations for significant achievements in the church.

The easiest solution, of course, is for the pastor to write a brief sermon or homily. This will not be as well read (if at all) as more personal and specific discussions of church issues or opportunities.

If a permanent location is needed for this feature, it

would be better placed on page two or three than on the front page. Readers will certainly want to see what the pastor has to say and will look for that contribution. (Whatever gets readers to turn the page helps.) Meanwhile, removal of the pastor's feature from page one enables you to use the most newsworthy items before you. In the rare case when it might be advisable to put the pastor's words on page one, a news-type headline should be used rather than something like, "The Pastor Says. . . ."

New members should be recognized with more than a listing of their names. Try to provide a background paragraph on each one; include present work and interests, family ties, full name, full address, and telephone number. If possible, print a picture.

A similar treatment of established members can be interesting, too. Such information is not well known, if at all, about most of our people. One or two individuals could be featured in each, or an occasional, issue.

Try to be as accurate as the local paper, and more, in reporting **deaths and marriages.** You will also need to report **births and baptisms,** with dates, and removals, graduations, special recognitions, and celebrations. These are news.

Except where they request not to be listed, for whatever reason, **those who are in hospitals** or ill should receive attention.

Seek out **new perspectives.** Do you know how a specific church program or practice is viewed by one or more of the older members, by an articulate teenager, by someone from another culture or country who is now a member—or by the janitor or sexton? Everybody would read what these people had to say.

Some **church classes and groups** are involved in lively and stimulating discussions of **major issues** of the day. Some of this could be shared with the congregation in brief comments on well-framed questions, rather than by trying to report on or summarize the course.

Members are entitled to being told promptly how their **fund-raising or special gifts campaigns** have fared; how they are doing in meeting budget requirements, with full disclosure; and what the statistics show about **membership,** attendance, and all the rest. Such information can be easily provided in formal listings with updated figures from issue to issue. Increasing numbers of official boards report their actions after each meeting. Even though this may not be earth-shaking, it should be encouraged.

I think it is unfortunate to speak of a "local" church (congregation or particular church is better). My objection is based on the fact that every church, by nature, has, or should have, a vision and outreach around the world. The newsletter can be a constant reminder of this, and can also be a corrective by reporting **denominational and ecumenical news**

from many sources—publications, news releases, missionary letters, and the local press. Most of all, the newsletter can do it by keeping firm the ties with a congregation's own missionaries in distant parts of the world, or even with acquaintances if the congregation does not have its "own" missionaries.

Letters to a church or pastor (with any too-personal references and errors removed) can be a helpful and interesting feature. Excerpts will be enough if a letter is long, but excerpts should be so indicated. (About the errors, for example, if the letter is written to "Reverend Janes," you would correct that to Mr. or Ms. Janes, just as you would any other error that should not be printed.)

These are a few of the many kinds of news sources and features available to a newsletter editor whose own experiences, contacts, and creativity will suggest many more.

On Copyrights

Church offices need to be especially aware of copyright regulations and the ethics involved. It is to be hoped that people are well informed about this subject in regard to reproducing lyrics or texts. Usually, the problem comes in last-minute decisions, with press time just ahead. It is not enough to use quotation marks and writer's name for anything more than a few sentences or a paragraph. Permission must be secured from the holder of the copyright, whose name appears usually on a left-hand page at a book's beginning. Except for a publication which is to be sold, such permission is usually given for use without any charge, but you must show that it is "used by permission" of the copyright holder.

With easy copying processes today, it is a great temptation to make copies of all kinds of material without permission or any indication of the source. By whatever fancy name this may be justified or camouflaged, it is not the way the church should operate.

Writing to Be Read

In this limited discussion, very little space is being devoted to the question of how to write what goes into a newsletter. It is desirable that the editor chosen for this responsibility be an experienced writer. Many good books on the subject are easily available, including *The Elements of Style*, by E. B. White and William Strunk, *The Way to Write* by John Fairfax and John Moat, and *The Art of Readable Writing* by Rudolph Flesch.

Editors will see to it that even in such abbreviated and condensed news items the basic who, what, when, where, why, and how of any good news story are honored. Every story should be checked to make sure that not one of these significant facts is omitted.

News items should lead off with a well-focused summary of the essentials. Subsequent sentences and paragraphs should fill out the details roughly in order of their importance.

Rewriting of most stories by the editor should be taken in stride. Even though stories are rewritten, they can still carry the by-line of the original writer. Modesty will restrain the editor from using his or her own by-line.

Light and Lively. . . .

Give your newsletter a light touch. It can and should be much more informal than your daily paper, and far more personal. Someone in your congregation is likely to have a fun-and-games hobby, with brain teasers and riddles (children of all ages love riddles). You may include light stories, limericks, and anecdotes. Think of what the *Reader's Digest* does along these lines. A puzzle or riddle or factual question of the month (or week) would attract interest.

Favorite recipes are a special item of interest for newsletters. And, to fill an inch or half-inch of space, you can keep a store of wise, humorous, probing quotations from past and present stores. Or you can use a suitable bit of art in those spaces.

Use Good, Good Pictures

Good pictures for a newsletter deserve a major emphasis. More and more duplicating and printing machines reproduce photographs well. Where you have access to such equipment, you will want to make the most of it. This means that you will insist on sharply focused black and white pictures with good contrasts; that you will use only those photographs that are well composed or those that can be cropped to bring out the point of central interest. Do not feel obligated to accept a dull, hazy, or poorly composed picture. Wait for a good one. Too many amateurs take pictures at a distance. Distant groups are hardly worth using unless, after cropping, a close-up results from enlargement. A poor picture is worse than no picture.

Cropping and Scaling

Study the pictures in your daily newspaper to see the results of good cropping—cutting out extraneous subjects and distractions so as to focus attention on the point of specific news interest. You will not be able to see how unbalanced or ill-composed it may have been originally, because cropping has taken care of that problem.

Use a ruler or T-square and a grease (or china-marking) pencil whose marks can be easily removed later with a tissue. If special care must be taken to avoid damage to the photograph, small strips of a gummed label can be placed along the edge (outside the space to be used) for the crop marks.

Since most of your pictures will be portraits, let me offer a few cautions. One, crop fairly close above the head. Two, include the neck, showing at least the knot in a man's necktie. Three, center the picture.

If an enlargement will help, have it made by your usual film processor. If you attach a picture with crop marks, the enlargement can usually be made within your marks, if you call special attention to them. You may have somone in your church who has a darkroom and equipment to make enlargements.

For church newsletters, portraits can usually be only slightly larger than a postage stamp, if they are cropped close. Sometimes they should be larger, so don't hesitate to use whatever will be appropriate and of news value.

If you have been given a picture of several people or a group taken at a distance, you will want to crop it close and have it enlarged to fill your available space. You would probably crop it to show subjects from the waist up.

Scaling—reduction or enlargement—of pictures is indicated by percentages. That is, if you want the photograph half its present size, mark it 50 percent, one-third, 33 percent, and so on.

It is important to have identifications on the backs of pictures, perhaps on a strip of a gummed label.

Here is an illustration of what cropping can do to help a

picture. In the full picture to the right, you may be distracted by the side of the house, the growing shrubs, the window, and the full canopy with its bold stripes. The cropped picture eliminates most of that, leaving enough of the stripes to identify the sand box canopy, but with the focus on the child.

Cropping: cutting out extraneous subjects and distractions so as to focus attention on the point of specific news interest. Mark the picture with a grease pencil or tape to show the area to be reproduced.

Scaling: changing the x size without changing the ratio of the dimensions of the original picture. The diagonal line method of scaling shows how you can reduce or enlarge any given picture.

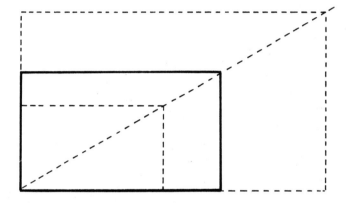

Focus on the child is increased by effective *cropping* of the original photograph.

Other Art Ideas

Line drawings, pen sketches, clip-sheet art, and illustrations can be well used in most duplicating processes. Well chosen and placed, they brighten and add interest to a page of type.

Don't overlook the art produced in children's church school classes. Samples can be reduced on your photocopier or by a commercial quick-print establishment. (A small city newspaper has a daily front-page feature next to the weather, a small miniature (2-by-1½-inches) reproduction of children's art from one of the local elementary schools.) This is a great feature just for the taking.

The Front Page

What is seen on the first page may well determine whether the rest of a newsletter is read. It is important to plan this page well.

The most important—newsworthy—stories of any issue should appear on the first page, with the very most important one usually at the top of the right-hand column under suitable headlines. I am assuming that each page has two or three columns for reasons discussed under "Use of Type."

It is better to have several stories on the front page than to have one long story, but it is not good to have several that are jumped (continued) onto a later page. It can be routine to begin a longer story in the middle or lower part of the right-hand column and run over to page two without including a line indicating this continuation. Readers understand that they are to turn a page.

Nothing helps a front page more than a good picture, a photograph, if it meets previously discussed specifications. It can relate to a news story on the front page, or elsewhere in the issue, or it can, with a few lines under it, tell its own story.

Reader interest can be drawn to inside pages by teaser (or bulletin) lines in rules on the front page, like the following.

To the right is a front page that exhibits many of the principles stressed here. The date, volume, and issue number are on the front page for quick reference. (You want to know that you are reading the latest issue.)

Notice the attention-getting sketch on peacemaking. It is usually better to have such sketches or pictures down in the story a few lines rather than at the top where you already have white space. But the story—one of five on the page—is a brief one. The 7-by-8½-inch page is full, but does not appear crowded. Headlines are strong enough for their respective stories. A photograph toward the bottom of column two would have made this an even more interesting page.

How to Produce It

We have come a long way from the time when most churches had little more than inefficient stencil printers or messy spirit duplicating processes. Today, even small offset presses are practical and often found in churches. Good typewriters with interchangeable elements for different type styles are easily available. Copying machines, from fairly simple to very complex and efficient, are in our churches or only a few steps away. If the quantity of printed impressions is not large, instant printing services, with a variety of capabilities, can often do our work for less than we can buy, pay the service charges, and maintain the necessary equipment.

Most equipment-selling establishments will allow a brief testing period for some kinds of copiers or printers before final purchase. This is desirable before you make a substantial investment in a process that may not be exactly what you need. Or if you see church printing that is well prepared and produced, you could make a visit to check out the processes and equipment being used. It is better to do that than to buy what the first salesman has to offer.

There is no good reason to have a typewriter that produces blurred or unclear copy. The purchase of an expensive new machine is not always necessary. Is there a first-class repair shop not far away where some keys or the rubber platen or rollers can be replaced? Good repairs are available within a reasonable distance everywhere.

Increasing numbers of churches are moving toward word processors or more complex computer systems. This is doubtless the coming trend for all except small churches that might not be able to justify the expense. But even for these, if there is an employed secretary, computer capability should be explored. With a good printer connected to the word processor (and there is a

---

RAPPORT

A Newsletter for Richmond Area Presbyterians

Vol. 3 No. 6   March-April, 1985

PEACE OFFERING TAKEN AT GRACE COVENANT

Grace Covenant took its first offering for peace, since signing the Commitment to Peacemaking last March, on Jan. 6, 1985, for $461.51. Hereafter this offering will be taken on Worldwide Communion Sunday, the first Sunday in October. Fifty percent of the offering was sent to the National Peacemaking Program, 25% was sent to Presbytery and Synod. The remaining 25% will be used at Grace Covenant for educational resources, speakers, and conferences, in an effort to enable its members to be more effective peacemakers.

BANNERS, ANYONE?

Anyone interested in making or working on banners carrying the RAP emphases for use at its meetings should call the coordinator, Aubrey Brown, at 358-6987 or 355-7449. Costs of material will be covered by RAP.

County Churches Meet Many Emergency Needs

Presbyterian churches in the counties surrounding Richmond have ready and efficient agencies through which to provide emergency assistance for needy individuals and families in addition to the respective Departments of Social Services.

Clothes, food, fuel, shoes, prescriptions, and other validated needs are made immediately available. In Chesterfield, it is the Chesterfield Volunteer Association, (748-0574), Box 844, Chester 23831; in Hanover, it is MCEF (emcef), Mechanicsville Churches' Emergency Fund, and in Henrico, ISH, Interfaith Services of Henrico (359-4411), 4912 W. Marshall St., Richmond 23230.

Ginter Park Youth Are Persuasive Lobbyists

With a bill before the Virginia General Assembly designed to exempt food merchants from paying a sales tax on unsold goods contributed to feed the needy, a group of the Ginter Park church's high school students were in the spotlight when they appeared before the House Finance Committee.

JonScott McClung, 13, speaking for the 20-member delegation and described by reporters as the youngest person ever to appear before a General Assembly body, told what they had seen of the needs at a place like Freedom House, a shelter for the homeless and hungry.

"What burns me up," he said, "is that when stores throw food away, they don't have to pay sales tax, but when they give it away to be eaten, they do."

The committee voted unanimously to change the existing provision and both the House and Senate approved the step.

LIVELY WEDNESDAY PROGRAM IS FEATURED AT WESTMINSTER

One of the popular features for retirees in the Richmond area is the "Soup 'n Sandwich" luncheon at Westminster church (4103 Monument Ave.) every second Wednesday. It begins at 11:30 a.m. with a social period, soup-sandwich lunch at noon, followed by an especially interesting program.

Frank Soden, popular sports and television personality, will be the March 13 speaker on "Experiences from Behind the Scenes in Radio and TV."

March will offer a trip to Washington, D.C., for a dramatic production.

April's program will focus on World War II memories, with John Moffatt as the speaker. In May there will be an overnight trip to Winston-Salem and a tour of the old Moravian village.

---

wide variety in the products of different printers), you can be sure to have a sharp, usable text for your newsletter and other needs.

Frequency

Most church newsletters are published on a once-a-month schedule. That seems to be about in line with an average congregation's available resources—i.e., editorial and news contributions and office or volunteer staff to produce, address, and prepare it for mailing. Once-a-month newsletters are obviously worth producing, or churches would not have them, but it is difficult to carry anything with significant news value on a monthly basis.

Larger churches, and those with adequate staff and volunteer help—including an editor who can stay on top of the job—have weekly newsletters. This is clearly the best arrangement where it is possible and where costs of production and mailing can be absorbed by office budget provisions.

Other churches publish a newsletter every two weeks or twice a month as a compromise between the advantages and disadvantages. Some churches publish a newsletter quarterly, and some, on an irregular schedule.

Size and Format

Since copying processes for standard-size sheets are easily available, most church newsletters are multiples of 8½-by-11 or 14-inch sheets, front and back of each. Space for mailing address, return address, and postal information is left open on the lower part of the outside sheet.

With a little more care and patience, these 11- and 14-inch sheets can be folded into booklet form. If more than one sheet is involved, stapling, an added step in the process, is necessary. Another standard size is an 11-by-17-inch sheet folded once to 8½-by-11-inch and folded once more for mailing.

Multiple flat sheets are the norm, folded finally for mailing, with any added inserts stapled inside. (An electric stapler is not expensive.) Several sheets and inserts can be included with no added cost in third-class mailing rates. With changing requirements, it is important to check this out with the nearby post office.

Before deciding on the paper to be used, enlist the help of a paper dealer or distributor to advise you in buying what you need and can best use at the most advantageous price. You will find that bond paper, twenty pound, is probably best. In some situations, paper suppliers will offer substantial savings if groups of churches combine their standing orders and arrange for their own storage or delivery schedule. Canvass all local paper supply houses to see what savings they can offer for quantity purchases. Repeat this procedure annually.

For most newsletters, twenty-pound bond is best. Heavier and more costly paper is not needed. Lighter weight (sixteen lb.) will allow the print to show through. Offset paper usually is not needed and will cost substantially more. If the page size needed is 8½-by-14-inch, there will be so much waste in cutting offset that the bill will be substantially higher. Bond paper of that size can be ordered and cut without waste. (For some uses where only one side is printed, sixteen pound may be useful; for other uses, you may need twenty-four pound bond or offset.)

Color Can Be Good—or Bad

Color can significantly enliven a page if it is used well. Color is best used for a spot or accent to give special emphasis. If colored ink is used to print type, it must be very dark. Pictures may well be ruined if printed in anything but black or almost black.

For easy readability, contrast is needed between ink and paper. The greatest contrast is between black and white, and the more that contrast is reduced, the more difficult it is to read a printed sheet.

Fortunately, changing colors on a press and cleaning up afterward are so troublesome that non-commercial printers will stick with black ink. But if, for example, green is desired for the Christmas season, the green should be as dark as you can make it.

If colored paper is used, and I think it should be, it should be a light rather than a dark color, even if black ink is used. Remember: Make the contrast sharp. It is a shame to see a well-written and designed newsletter made difficult, if not almost impossible, to read because of an ill-considered printing job.

Use of Type

Another key to making a newsletter readable is the choice and use of type. With word processors and printers, we now have an almost unlimited selection of type styles and sizes for our use. Fancy or unusual type should be avoided for anything but an occasional emphasis. The main body type for newsletters should be no smaller than typewriter pica type. Anything with all capitals should be avoided except for headlines and special emphasis. Italics are good for an emphasized word, sentence, or brief paragraph, but scarcely more. The same goes for script and other unusual type faces.

It is easy for a typist to type newsletter lines all the way across a page. Unfortunately, that is also a way to lose a reader's attention. Tests show that we do not read single lines of type easily if they have more than fifty characters (and spaces) in them.

Therefore, it is better to plan for two (or three) columns to a page. This breaks up the type better and allows for more white space and inserted illustrations.

Long paragraphs and solid blocks of type are hard to read. A good many things can be done to make reading easier:

— An occasional paragraph of one or two sentences can be made a half-inch narrower than the ones before and after it—for example, indent from right and left.
— An extra line of space can be inserted.
— The first word (or two) can be in all-caps and flush left, with the next line, but only the next line, indented two or three spaces.
— The first two or three words can be underscored.
— Underlined subheads, flush left, can be inserted with space left above and below them.
— An announcement, quotation, or brief item can be boxed and inserted in the column unless this causes an awkward break in the story.
— At the bottom of a column, a three- or four-line item can be used with rules above and below. This item can be in bold or a special type face. Or a good quotation can be used in italics, with rules.
— For longer feature articles, if you are having type set by a printer, an inserted larger initial (18 or 24 point) letter can be used, with the rest of the firstword in all caps. This style is not

— appropriate for news items.
— For a series in a list, or to call attention, use a bullet (like a solid •) to introduce the line, just as dashes are used in this series.

Remember: Readers are not compelled to read what we produce for them. We must make it easy and attractive.

Names Are Important

The name of a newsletter can be an asset. It's worth extra effort to seek and find "the best" possible one. You may then want to have a capable artist design a masthead with a distinctive logo. This will nearly always be placed at the top of the front page, but, for a change, it is good to use it in other first-page locations. Along with the name should be such basic information, such as: The church's name, address, and telephone number. If churches are located at intersections of a well-known street and one not so well known, it is very important to list the number on the well-known street. I believe it is also important to list both streets because visitors and most residents may not know how far out the location is on the better-known street. So, you can say your address is, for example, 4200 Mulberry Street at Hastings.

With the masthead should also be the issue date, the volume number, and the issue number. The volume number includes those published within a twelve-month period. Each issue published within that period has its own successive number. It is important (to librarians and archivists) to keep the numbering right. The date (and name) may also be repeated on each page. Also, be sure to number the pages.

The editor's name and telephone number should be listed. Occasionally, it is appropriate to list, alongside the church's address, the name and telephone number of the pastor and of the church secretary, and, sometimes, of the entire church staff.

Here are the names of some newsletters that come to me regularly:

The Witness	Second Press
The Messenger	Laurel Gazette
The Church Mouse	Bethlehem Star
(Church name) Highlights	
Progress	The Tie
The Outreach	(Denominational name) Connection
Tuckahoe Torch	New Covenant Rainbow
Forest Hill Family	Crestwood Chronicle
The Piper	(Church name) News
Grace Notes (from Grace Covenant Church)	5th Avenue Voice

Who Should Get It—and How?

There is no substitute for prompt, direct mailing to a regular church list. Many church lists are now computerized and can be kept up-to-date. All lists need to be corrected for each mailing. When addresses carry a line stating that address correction is requested, the post office will provide the information, changing the originator each time. The cost is no longer small and it is increasing, but it may be the most efficient way to keep a church list current and to avoid sending mail where there is no recipient.

Smaller churches with no mechanical addressing capability can easily maintain a master list for reproduction on 8-by-11-inch sheets of gummed labels in eleven-name columns, three columns to a page.

Postal requirements call for a minimum of two hundred identical pieces of mail in order to claim the cheaper, non-profit third-class postal rate. It would be more economical to add as many as fifty names to a list in order to meet the two hundred minimum requirement than to pay a higher postage rate. There are better reasons for adding an additional number of recipients to a mailing list. Here are suggestions of people who would appreciate your newsletter:

• Membership prospects
• Visitors to the church
• Devoted and special members who have moved away. (This list should be re-examined and pruned from time to time. You do not want to encourage anyone who has moved away to keep a paper membership in a hometown church.)
• Former pastors
• Students away at college or in military service
• Neighborhood churches
• Denominational colleagues or officials
• Certain local civic and community leaders and social service workers
• Perhaps a real estate firm or agent particularly knowledgeable about your part of town
• A half-dozen or more churches similar to yours (This list could well be changed from time to time to establish a variety of contacts. The address plate should say: PLEASE EXCHANGE.)

Sending an occasional (marked) copy to your local paper's religion editor is probably better than having that editor on the regular mailing list, thus avoiding piled-up, unread mail that eventually goes into "File 13."

Second-Class Mailings. Second-class postal rates are less expensive than first class, but they require compliance with a printed (and post officeapproved) mailing schedule. That is, if your printed postal entry says that you publish weekly, you must do so. There are also differences in how the mailing is prepared for the post office. To avoid mistakes and unnecessary labor, it is always best to check carefully with the postal clerks to be sure all instructions are clear and understood.

An envelope for either kind of mailing (second- or third-class) is unnecessary and may well be an impediment and added expense. There are two advantages: The newsletter is protected from soil or damage in transit, and the addressing chore can be done ahead of time. However, inserting the newsletter in an envelope is an added and unnecessary step. Most churches leave the lower part of the last page of the newsletter for the address and other post office-required information. The space for the address, the form of the postal entry, and other items need post office approval.

THE CHURCH DIRECTORY

A church directory can be a very importat contribution to the life of a congregation. In most cases directories are produced in the church office by the staff. Sometimes they are typed according to specifications and printed in book form commercially.

In such directories will be found staff names, officers, committee and choir members, and organizational leaders, all with addresses and telephone numbers (home and work). Sometimes you will find a thumbnail history of the church, information about ecclesiastical relationships from local to national levels, and perhaps descriptive matter about the church's program and outreach or committee areas of responsibility.

The major, and most important, part of the book consists of active members' names, alphabetically by families, first names of adults and children, with both home and business telephone numbers and street addresses.

It is routine and easy to show grade-levels of children through college or graduate school years by a code system. For example, K is for Kindergarten; the

numbers 1–12 show school grade as of that year, 13 for college freshman, G. S. for graduate student. For pre-school children, date of birth is shown. If members are in zone or Shepherd Care groups, the number in parentheses can be used.

Other useful features in a directory include a listing of "Who to Call" about all kinds of church-related needs and the numbers of community agencies and institutions, which church members should have conveniently at hand.

It is of the greatest importance to be sure that the typed names and numbers are not reduced to a size too small to be easily read and that the listings are printed in black ink on paper that is white or no darker than a light tint. Much, much detailed and careful work goes into the preparation of a directory, and the printing of it in small type on dark paper should not be allowed to make it difficult to read.

A convenient size for such a directory is 5½-by-8½ inches, made from 8½-by-11-inch sheets folded once. A cover with the name of the church, the year, and any suitable picture or sketch will provide a note of distinction. The church's telephone number may be printed in larger type (perhaps 14- or 18-point) and in bold face on the cover.

More ambitious and useful is a pictorial directory. Most churches would produce the usual pictorial directory no more often than once in five years or so. It is a complicated and demanding chore, but the result is well worth it.

These directories are often provided without cost to participating churches for the privilege of selling photographs to the members whose pictures are taken. One photographer in this kind of enterprise is Olan Mills of Columbia, South Carolina.

The book produced has a color photograph of the church on the glossy cover. Inside are color photographs, by family groups or by singles, arranged alphabetically. Following the pictures will be found all family and single names, addresses, and telephone numbers.

In contracting to produce such a directory, the photographer is permitted to seek to sell to the respective members copies of photographs that are taken, but not to use undue pressure in so doing.

The major problem comes in arranging for a concentrated schedule—first to have the picture taken, then to reschedule those who fail to appear, all fitting in with the photographer's available time. A final round of schedules involves everybody's selection from the proofs of the pictures to be used. Volunteers, not members of a church staff, must be enlisted to take care of all of this, following through to remind those who fail to appear. The result of all of this will be an attractive and useful volume of which you will be proud.

Tying People Together

LETTERS AND NOTES

With all the wonders of electronic wizardry and the complex printing and duplicating processes at our disposal, can any communications capability match the simple writing of a letter or a note? If it is handwritten rather than typed, and therefore more personal, a letter is all the more appreciated, even though the writer's penmanship is not the best.

Even better than the best possible compliment going out the church door after a sermon is a brief note saying hardly more than, "Your clear explanation of how God helps us deal with our doubts was just what I needed," or, "I want to find a place in my church life where I can be of help to some lonely people. Your sermon helped me in trying to think about this."

Telephone calls and visits are appreciated when one is in a hospital, but a brief note written on a card (it does not have to be a special or "store-bought" card) may be treasured forever if a couple of written lines say something like, "You are important to me and to all of us—and very much in my prayers. Your brave witness in a time of trouble strengthens my faith in God." Little notes like that would be good for anybody, in a hospital or not.

Most of us feel that we don't know what to say to friends in the face of a loss by death. We don't need to. What is important is to show that we are supportive, standing by them. A couple of lines saying somthing like, "My heart goes out to you in your great loss," is all that is needed and is better than costly flowers that will soon fade. The words of the note will not fade. Multiply something like this across the disappointments, losses, and hardships experienced in any congregation and it becomes clear how we can help others bear up and grow strong in anxious times.

The most prodigious letter writer I have ever known misses few opportunities within a wide circle of friends and acquaintances of several generations. On special occasions and no special occasions she writes. Following a meeting of her women's circle each month, she mails a copy of the special newsletter to each absentee, with a few personal lines added to tell about what happened at the meeting and to say how much the absentee was missed.

With all the protective and defensive walls we build around ourselves, it is not easy for us to be aware of one

another's deep stresses and impending crises. Sometimes, it becomes appropriate to let these things be known in small groups. In some churches, in an informal service, it is possible to share a need for prayer or support. In some, it is possible to write specific prayer requests on cards in the pews. These are collected during the singing of the first hymn as ushers come slowly up the aisles to receive them and carry them forward for use in the pastor's morning prayer.

One does not have to have a special gift to make an appreciated contact with a stranger or newcomer to a community. It would be regarded as something far more than routine if you wrote a note saying, "Let me stop by and take you to church with me tomorrow." That you would take the time and trouble to write and mail the note says a great deal. Something like that, without being too pushy or condescending, can be used to help reclaim individuals and families who have drifted away, who have gone through catastrophic troubles, or who may never have indicated an interest in church affairs. A sincerely written and appropriately timed note can bring healing and resotoration.

(*Note:* The use of larger mailings is discussed in Using Direct Mail, pp 42.)

A *Pastor's Notes and Letters*

I was once shown a pastor's letter of encouragement in a time of need that has been kept as a treasure for many years. I saw the interest and responsiveness stimulated in a high school graduate's family by such attention. And I wondered if any comparable investment of time or attention could have been more worthwhile.

The best example of the practice of note writing is a pastor who used a simple printed card saying, "A Friendly Word." On this card he wrote one or two sentences on a Sunday afternoon and mailed it to each visitor who had been in church that morning. Such personal and prompt attention drew that pastor and those who received his attention very close across the years. That same card, with its printed inscription, went to countless others—to those in the hospital awaiting an operation, to those facing a difficult problem, to those receiving a special honor or even attention in the newspaper.

With word processors and the insertion of personal names and references, it is possible to use even typed letters to write to high school and college graduates or other special groups related to the church.

All of this is not to lay added burdens on pastors who already have more than they can accomplish. It is simply a reminder that where the necessary help and mechanical ability are available, even such attentions that are not hand-written can have a significant effect in forming close ties between a pastor and a congregation.

If love begets love, as I know it does, such a writing ministry by a pastor will surely stimulate those who receive warm, friendly, and encouraging letters to join the company and write their own.

REACHING OUT BY TELEPHONE

The first point of church contact by telephone, the receptionist, is usually the secretary. A receptionist's alertness, pleasant tone, unhurried manner, and ability to listen and get it right the first time are characteristics that do much to project a favorable impression of a church. Turning a church business call into an extended social visit can help to tie up the line or absorb a secretary's valuable time unnecessarily. Members (as well as secretaries) need to be aware of this.

It is certainly better manners on the part of a caller to say who is calling, but it is not appropriate for a receptionist to ask, "May I say who is calling?" There are important, if not necessary, occasions when the caller does not want any intermediary to know who is calling. And to think that the identity of the caller may have something to do with whether the call will be accepted raises all kinds of negative images. I am aware that telephone sales pitches and other nuisance calls may need to be screened, but there must be better ways of doing it. It may be important to let it be known that except for emergencies, a pastor's study time should not be interrupted. Notices can indicate the better times to call the pastor, but people should not be made too fearful about interrupting.

There are innumerable good ways in which pastors use the telephone, limited only by what is in good taste and effective. Whether a regularly recorded message or prayer of hope and encouragement is offered may be determined by the temper of the community and/or how many similar recordings are being made and used. Brief tests, with adequate publicity, can determine the need or opportunity.

Pastoral Care Opportunities

Pastoral care and new-member committees can make a variety of good uses of the telephone. It is my opinion that church members should be more strongly encouraged to call those who are ill in homes and hospitals than to visit them. It may be that only those with very close ties should do the visiting. A telephone call has several advantages for the one who is ill. A call can be more easily terminated than a personal visit. It can be shorter and less tiring. The ill person may be able to initiate the call. A visit by telephone can insure the visitor against an unwelcome intrusion (though even a telephone call should first be tested to see if it is appropriate). Telephone calls can be repeated several times during a hospital stay.

Since many ill persons would prefer a telephone call over a visit, it would be helpful if church newsletter and bulletin listings included telephone numbers. One caring

congregation that does well in keeping in close touch with members who are ill provides a list at each Wednesday evening fellowship dinner. Two names on the list are highlighted for notes and greetings in a given week. On each table are note-sized cards for a few words of good cheer and support. These notes are collected and are taken to the designated persons the next day by a pastor or visitor.

Another widely practiced custom is the assignment of individuals (often older members) to make daily telephone calls to individuals living alone who want to be checked on in this way. This is simply to see how they are doing, if they need anything, and to exchange friendly words of encouragement and support. Members on these lists are there because they have signed up for the attention and have given names and telephone numbers of persons to be called if there is no answer. They should also let it be known where a key is to be found if entrance to the home is necessary.

A Telephone Network

A telephone tree or network can be an important communications medium. This enables an entire congregation to be reached with urgent information as quickly as possible. A supervisor or director of the system recruits captains who are responsible for calling five persons, each one of whom will be given the responsibility for five more homes, thus covering the entire membership.

Few things say more about a church than how its members rally around a family when a death occurs, making sure that everyone knows, that out-of-town family members and friends are cared for, that, in many cases, a meal is provided for the family and their connections at the church or in a home before or after the service. An established plan of telephone contacts can make this possible.

These are a few of the ways in which an alert and sensitive pastoral care committee in a congregation can make good use of the telephone. Such committees will think of many others. New-member committees will experiment and discover effective means of welcoming newcomers to a community and, when appropriate, offer to come by for them for worship the next day or for another church event. Any number of members are lost to churches because their absences are not noticed until, finally, they have been allowed to drift away. Many times a friendly telephone call to let people know that they have been missed can be used to sustain interest and relationships. Promoters of special events who want to make sure that attendance is good can do hardly anything that is as effective as calling individuals and giving them personal and cordial invitations, with all the overtones of friendliness.

FELLOWSHIP OPPORTUNITIES

Welcoming Visitors

Few concerns have a better pay-off in churches than friendly, instead of perfunctory, attention to visitors and newcomers. While most of this depends on having at least a few individuals who are friendly and outgoing by nature or commitment, who are always looking out for strangers, who will see to it that more than nominal or "proper" welcome is extended, some of it must come from tradition. Friendly and outgoing people attract other friendly and outgoing people, and together they help to develop a loving and caring congregation.

It is an oft-told story that individuals can go into strange congregations, join in the worship and leave without being spoken to by anyone other than an official greeter or usher who has time to say little more than "Good morning" as he or she shakes hands. Church members, including the best of them, are often so involved with longtime friends and associates that they seldom think of visitors and newcomers. The habit of being warm and friendly to visitors is one to cultivate, because evidence suggests that many people who join a church do so because someone saw to it that they were introduced to a considerable number of those who were already members.

Registration blanks in the pews provide one of the best and easiest methods of discovering visitors. These blanks are usually kept at one end of the pew. At a designated time in the service, they are *returned* to their original places. On the return, it is expected that each person in the pew will look at the list, identify anyone not known before, and see if any signer is not a member. With that information, friendly greetings can be extended after the service, and the visitor can be taken in tow for introductions to a number of others, especially if a coffee or social hour follows.

Even though some visitors seem to try to slip into and out of church without being greeted, they are the exception. Most visitors welcome friendly greetings and feel slighted if they fail to receive them. Any church profits from a reputation of friendliness.

One of the best greeters I have known has a well-designed strategy. When new members are announced, she is ready to write their names on a bulletin or scrap of paper to help her remember when she speaks to them after the service. When she meets a new person at church, she writes the name down as soon as she gets home, or sooner. When a visitor appears, she makes sure that several members are introduced and are told something of the new person's work or interests. At any gathering in the church, she can be seen moving from one person to another, with special attention to those who may be new or visiting.

She doubtless knows and is known by more members of her church than anyone else.

Multiplying the number of such open and friendly members will strengthen the witness and enhance the reputation of any church.

Sunday Coffee Hours

In developing a friendly, caring congregation, much will depend upon providing different levels and contexts in which communication can take place. Sunday school classes and organized societies for different age and other groups have long afforded major opportunities.

What about the considerable number of people in any church who seem to want to confine their church relationships almost solely to what happens in their pew on Sunday morning? A coffee hour between Sunday school and the beginning of worship may be the best or only possibility of providing an opportunity for fellowship in this case, but it does have limitations. In the churches where I see this social time working best, it is scheduled for after worship with considerable care and preparation. This calls for a modification of the "rush-for-home-after-church" attitude on the part of members and visitors who can then be drawn together over a cup of coffee, tea, or punch (with what is suitable for children) in an unhurried, friendly situation that promotes and enhances acquaintance and interchange.

The setting can significantly contribute through attractively arranged tableware and the use of cups and saucers instead of plastic. If planners are seen to take the opportunity seriously, others are more likely to do so. It is not left to chance to make sure that friendly greeters and servers are in place to help everyone feel at home and to see to it that special attention is paid to visitors. Where this is done well, clock time becomes relatively unimportant; conversations continue in an unhurried manner and at a level seldom surpassed elsewhere in a church's life.

Most churches can take much more advantage of their grounds. For good weather days in spring, summer, and early fall, setting up a table or two in shaded areas contributes to the "after church" possibilities. This makes it easier for some persons who do not usually participate in this weekly social exchange. The outdoor location does something else that is significant. It shows to the neighborhood and those in passing cars the picture of a church where members enjoy one another's fellowship, and it advertises appropriately and powerfully the spirit of a friendly church family.

Weekday Opportunities

Another special opportunity for deeper communication among church members (and friends or prospective

members who may be invited) is in the midweek gathering, usually held on Wednesday evening.

An emphasis on fellowship, a good meal (by whatever process the church uses), and a high quality program of interest for as many as possible is within the capabilities of every church and well worth the effort. Making the thirty to forty minutes before dinner a time of social interchange and special interest is a valuable opening. A simple appetizer, well-planned shared interests and skills by a variety of individuals can have far-reaching effects in deepening friendships and creating fellowship and good communication within a congregation.

SMALL GROUPS

Small group gatherings are as old as the church, beginning with the original twelve apostles. In recent years, we have seen a variety of ways in which small group procedures can be used to advantage in congregations. The potential values are so great, in my judgment, that no church should overlook or minimize them.

Many patterns are followed, and available books tell all about them. Most small groups meet once a month, except in vacation time, in members' homes. There is almost always a meal, with hosts providing the main dish and all others bringing agreed upon dishes.

What the groups do in unhurried evenings varies widely from church to church and from group to group, with each group usually determining its own procedures. Each host may determine what is done that evening.

Membership in the groups should be limited to a year, with names then re-drawn and re-assigned, with regard for singles, ages, gender, and, perhaps, proximity, though that is least important. Groups should have fourteen to twenty persons in them. The same persons should not be in groups together in successive years, insofar as that is possible.

I am stressing this pattern here because of my conviction that it offers an opportunity for significant communication at a greater depth and over a longer period than is normally available to us. It also provides what may be the most important element in communication—an opportunity to learn how to LISTEN.

Most of us can improve our listening ability immensely. Let me propose a test. When someone is telling us about an important incident or experience, while we are quiet and appear to be listening, what are we really doing? Most of us are thinking about something similar, or more exciting, that happened to us and are watching for the first chance to break in and tell about it. If we were asked, we would doubtless justify our interruption by saying that it establishes a bond, a point of identification, between us. It does nothing of the kind. Instead, we divert attention from the speaker to ourselves. This may give us a degree of satisfaction as we tell our story, but it is frustrating, demeaning, and perhaps even devastating, for we have pushed the other

person from the center of the stage and taken over. It is surprising to see this happening in the conduct of some people trained as counselors. They can hardly wait to take over.

If we are good listeners, we will continue to ask questions, to seek more information. We will press for details and express interest and concern, but we will leave the other person in control, at least for a reasonable amount of time before we try to tell our story. We may never get an opportunity to tell our story or make our point, but we will have done something far more important in our relationship with someone else. If you will think about how it makes you feel when someone really gives you a chance to unfold, who demonstrates genuine interest in you, then you will know that this is true.

Karl Menninger has said very perceptively that listening is a magnetic and strange thing, a creative force. He says that the friends who listen to us are the ones we move toward, and the ones we want to be around. Menninger claims that when we are listened to, we "unfold and expand." In his words, we must listen with affection to anyone who talks to us. People show us their souls. People who will show us their true selves, will be wonderfully alive.

When groups have members who can learn and teach each other to listen rather than to dominate, divert, or control the conversation, something very important can happen. Something below the purely superficial will begin to emerge, and new dimensions in communication can be established.

Using Non-print Media

TAPE AND VIDEO RECORDINGS

Cassette recordings of Sunday services, or at least the sermon, are provided as an appreciated ministry by many churches. Every church seems to have enough teenagers knowledgeable about electronics who can take charge of this. If the tapes are taken promptly to shut-ins or to those with special interests who may have been absent, ties are strengthened, and those who receive the attention are given another reason to know that they are being thought about and are considered valued members of the congregation.

Cassette recordings can do a great deal more. They can be used to send greetings or songs or a dramatization by children or other groups. A vivid imagination is not needed to understand how much this gift can mean to a member or friend of the church who is alone, ill, or shut in.

With video equipment in increasing numbers of homes, added dimensions are possible, especially in view of the relative low cost of video tapes. Video recorded messages sent to college students, members in military service, sponsored missionaries, and others open many doors.

With the increasing recognition of oral history possibilities, I cannot overemphasize the importance of recording voices, faces, and ideas of church members to preserve for future generations. This is especially true of all kinds of special events and celebrations when such recordings should be made.

The growing use of video tape in teaching and the prospect of its increasing significance are so extensive and specialized that I will not attempt to explore that area here.

AUDIO-VISUALS

There is no doubt that the powerful communication medium of our time is audio-visuals, for adults as well as for children. We neglect this medium at our peril. In the church, generally, we are just beginning to recognize its pervasive influence.

The field is so large, and expanding, and the procedures are so technical that adequate treatment of the how-to's would require a book instead of a section in a work like this. But to omit this brief comment would suggest that this writer is in the middle of a major

communications revolution of which he is not even aware!

Major church publishing houses have produced, and are constantly producing, all kinds of practical helps in this field. Resources for guidance are almost unlimited. Individuals in every church can take advantage of these resources, equipping themselves and keeping up with the best advances being made. Below are just a few ideas.

Some members of almost any church will have a store of 8 mm. family films. Among those films there are probably some taken on special church, or other, occasions which might be copied on a video cassette for historical or program use. Many individuals are, or will be, transferring everything they have on 8 mm. to videotape, and selections may be made more easily after the transfer.

Here, again, let me re-emphasize the standard of high quality for pictures—and sound. We are all accustomed to seeing and hearing what has been produced by experts, such as what's on television, so select only the very best recordings for a church project. This applies as well to photographs from travels, even to important and historic sites, and to recordings that may have been made for the record. Poorer quality material may be kept for the church's history, but do not inflict these on a gathering as part of a program.

When professionally produced 16 mm. films are projected, the largest available screen should be used, and the projector should be placed so that the image *fills*

the screen. Where possible, the sound for such films should always be fed into the room or auditorium sound system so as to take full advantage of your best fidelity. This assures good distribution of the sound across the room, instead of having it coming indistinctly from a distant corner.

When videotapes are used, enough television sets should be used so as to have sound and images within easy range of all the viewers.

With the prevalence of video equipment in so many if not most homes, it appears that the big advances will be in that medium. The relatively low cost of tapes and the explosive growth of videotape libraries and sales give a hint of the future potential for video.

The development of cable television and the opening up of public access channels add new dimensions as well. It may be some years before more than a few congregations are able to take full advantage of this technology, but combining resources from several churches could open the way toward meeting this opportunity.

Church supply houses and others are making more videotapes available. Congregations will find many programs appropriate for use over the cable system. Any videotapes should be examined with special care to make sure they are suitable for a particular church. The pressure for sales and rentals will no doubt be great, regardless of whether the advertised tapes are appropriate and true-to-fact.

BULLETIN BOARDS

Bulletin boards are defined here as those found inside churches, in hallways or at "traffic intersections" and gathering places. Outdoor signs and boards are discussed later.

From my observation and experience, despite the fact that every church is sure to have at least one bulletin board, I am convinced that most of these are not as effective as people believe. Unfortunately, some people feel they have promoted and publicized a coming program or event if they have stuck an announcement on a bulletin board. That can be a costly delusion.

When we did not have easy copying processes or newsletters and bulletins, posting a notice on a bulletin board may have been more effective. It was one of few tools available. That day has passed. Today, pinning an announcement to a bulletin board may be worse than doing nothing! It is worse than doing nothing if it causes you to feel that you have done something highly effective in promoting an important program.

Most churches do have permanently mounted boards, and they will continue to be used. I offer here some suggestions for making them as useful as possible.

Bulletin boards usually are mounted too high on the wall. If they are to be permanently mounted, place them low enough for readers wearing bifocals to read the printed matter and for older children to see without difficulty.

It is far better to have portable boards that can be placed on easels at convergence points of traffic and activity—where lines will be forming, where people usually gather to talk, and where there is good light, if not a spotlight. (A church does well to have several easels for a variety of uses. In addition to formal bulletin boards, poster boards with mounted pictures or announcements, various types of plywood, wallboard, and even heavy cardboard and other materials can be used to advantage.)

What should be put on these boards? Anything of special interest or information that cannot be used in the newsletter. Eye-catching posters may be mounted, though these will usually be used to better advantage on walls. If pictures of new members are not printed in the newsletter, post them on the board with identifications. Larger pictures taken at church events or in promotion of a forthcoming program do well. Newspaper clippings and pictures featuring church members are suitable, even though mentions are carried in the newsletter. Other suggestions may be found in the next section on displays and exhibits.

How the material is arranged and emphasized is important. A strong or focused light has already been mentioned as a primary concern. An arrow cut from colored paper can direct attention to a notice. A contrasting background makes a mounted picture or notice stand out. String or ribbon held by pushpins or thumbtacks offers a good way to suspend items that cannot be attached to a flat surface if you don't have hooktape. Masking and transparent tape are essential materials. Velcro in a variety of colors enlarges possibilities. A caution: Whatever is placed on the board should ordinarily be removed within a week if the board is to attract the interest of those passing by.

DISPLAYS AND EXHIBITS

Well planned displays and exhibits can be very effective in promoting, or as a part of, special events, celebrating major anniversaries, sharing the results of individual and group endeavors, honoring persons or organizations, recognizing and publicizing good activities and services, and much more.

A suggestion: When you go to fairs or commercial events where there are many exhibitors, make it a practice to take a few mental or written notes about what seems to attract the crowds or get desired participation. Some of these, of course, will not be suitable for church use. Others will be instructive. Among other discoveries, you will find such components as:

— Good lighting, without uncomfortable glare, to illuminate and focus attention
— An orderly, unified, eye-catching arrangement,

sometimes with moving objects, with effective use of color or, at least, contrasts
— Engaging, friendly, and outgoing people attending the exhibit. They are standing—not sitting, eager, and ready to talk, explain, answer questions, or show how something works.
— An offer of information, or an item that will be of interest or value
— Something about food, even if it is no more than a recipe or sample
— An opportunity to participate in a contest, a poll, or survey, or to share information
— Something to do with your hands or to test skill or aptitude
— Two or three chairs in a carpeted area where you may sit for awhile to rest or talk things over.

In short, the best planners show that they are thinking about *you*, what interests or concerns you and what you like to do or think about, have, or participate in. Whatever there is to show or sell is made to fit into that framework.

Whichever of these (or others that you see working) that are appropriate to the church's methods and motivations can put you on the road to planning, constructing, and operating an exhibit or display that has a good chance of achieving your objectives.

The Nuts and Bolts

You begin with your assigned (or selected) **space**—floor, table, or wall. If you can select the space, make sure of good visibility (where everybody can see it), the traffic pattern (where most people will pass or gather), and good lighting or electrical outlets.

Once situated, you plan to call attention to a well-focused message, such as participation in a coming anniversary, a vacation Bible school, or a trip to a church institution.

You will add **color** with paint, cloth hangings, banners, or costumes. A dull or cluttered background can be blocked out by a two- or three-paneled screen borrowed from a home or shop.

If a church does not have a two- or three-panel screen, perhaps covered with green or brown burlap, some members might have them in their homes for utility or decorator purposes. Some of these **screens** would likely be suitable for loan for a special showing—screening out distractions or providing surfaces for displays. If a church does not possess one, it would be good to construct one as a work-day project or commission a willing-to-help handyman to make one to be covered with burlap or contact paper. It would be a useful property.

What you have to say will be limited to **short, action-packed words,** pointing to desired results, all positive.

Viewers must be able to see and understand quickly what the display is all about. Something about the display had better be interesting or appealing enough to draw viewers into it. Make sure that the misuse of lights or color won't make the display difficult to read.

Leave no doubt about **what viewers are to do** after visiting your display: write a letter, make a telephone call, buy a book, sign up for a trip, etc. If the exhibit is being run without an attendant, print directions on an easy-to-read card or play them on a repeating recording.

Every church and/or community has individuals who have a variety of skills and experience that can be useful in planning, designing, constructing, and operating displays and exhibits. Enlisting their talents and interests is not difficult, since many of them have entirely too few opportunities to use their special gifts.

Every church has its full share of amateur photographers. Many may see nothing more to taking a picture than pressing a button, but you can seek out those who really understand how to take a professional-quality picture. Explore other **sources of good pictures,** too—posters, magazines, libraries, museums, corporate public relation offices, and travel agencies. Most likely, someone in your church has an eye for these things and collects them.

It is helpful if you can find someone who is able to make enlargements of pictures. Sometimes you may want one as big as 24" x 36". These are also available by mail order at modest cost; look for ads in magazines or big city newspapers.

If you don't have an artist to do your **lettering,** you can find stencils in many sizes in art or school supply stores, or you can use someone able to letter simply and neatly. Just be sure to have the letters big and strong enough with good contrast between the letters and the background.

It is amazing, if not inspiring, to see what people have in their basements, attics, dresser drawers, and scrapbooks. Most people are happy to donate if they know you need a particular item for an indicated purpose. You can also keep an eye open where you shop for discarded displays. Once they serve their purposes in the store, many are free for the taking. With a little ingenuity and a few touches of paint, they can serve a variety of uses.

Big cartons or sheets of cardboard can be easily notched and put together **to make a four-section display.** Two sheets of cardboard of the same size can be fitted together for a four-section display, providing eight usable sides. At the middle line on each sheet, cut vertically halfway up, press one sheet over the top of the other until the cut edges of the top sheet reach the surface on which the sheets are placed. A piece or two of masking or other tape may be used for security. Spray paint or other covering may be used as desired. Explore display houses and art supply stores in your area for materials and ideas.

Although **banners** are available everywhere, they can be used even better than they are. Don't just hang them on a wall and forget about them. With whatever suitable message or symbol attached, they can be hung from a pole and placed where they will serve the greatest purpose. They can be hung on wires dropped from the ceiling or out from the wall at a 90° angle in a general meeting room or, in some cases, in the sanctuary. For a special need, you can request your best banner-maker to design and make one to specifications.

With the wide variety of **audio-visual equipment** and materials available, there are possibilities for movement, color, sound, and music of the highest quality in a display. Think what you can do to add interest to an exhibit with tape-recorded comments and photographs of persons who attend or are well-known to your church. One caution: Moderate the volume of the sound.

Missions, stewardship, and other themes can be enlivened by good photographs, films, slides, videotapes, and other materials from national church headquarters, if reservations are made in time.

More help with displays and exhibits is available in your library, including a publication entitled *Display and Exhibit Handbook* (William Hayette, Inc.).

Planning and Promoting
Special Events and Celebrations

Well planned special events and celebrations open up opportunities and reveal interests and skills that routine programs may never reveal. There can be too many events, but more churches seem to have too few. And all of us have probably been to church celebrations of anniversaries, even of centennials, where we wondered why anything at all was done if it had to be so poorly. planned and executed. How can we make the most of these opportunities?

Celebrations can express a hearty thank-you for long, loyal, and generous service. They can honor or recognize someone's special or distinguished achievement or contribution. They can highlight an anniversary and, in doing so, deepen loyalties, teach history, and draw a congregation together around traditional values. They can enlarge a church's appreciation through arts and music festivals, reaching out and recognizing the skills and talents of many individuals in the community. They can launch or help to inaugurate a major new emphasis or program in a church's life. They can provide an occasion of fun and fellowship, drawing a congregation closer together, as in an annual picnic, retreat, or day of games and recreation.

Time and place are basic considerations. Be sure to consult a community calendar in order to avoid conflicting events. Especially in a small community, a football game or a basketball tournament would provide too much competition.

Church anniversaries need good advance planning, probably as much as two years, especially in signing-up major speakers and guests. Since the planning process itself holds significant values, it should not be rushed. This is a time to enlist the energies, interests, and special talents of every possible individual. When the time has been set, efforts should be made to get the date listed everywhere that it will make a difference and where support and cooperation will be needed. Most church events will be held in the church, but reservations may be required at a public park, recreational facility, hotel, restaurant, or hall.

Church members should be kept up-to-date with occasional bulletins or special notices as plans develop. Their interest and participation can and should be enlisted in every possible way. A major test of the success of any celebration is the number of people who participate as well as the quality of their involvement. Everyone has something to share and will be better off and happier through sharing. So, make it easy to get suggestions and feed back from everybody.

ANNIVERSARIES

Celebrations of anniversaries, especially centennials, need careful planning by hard-working and creative people. When the date and general outline have been set and the major speaker engaged, begin inviting former pastors and families, offering local hosts. The same provision should be made for those who have gone from the congregation into full-time church vocations.

It is worth a major effort to get addresses of all former members. This can be done through their friends in the church and community, but it is not easy. Many people can and should be assigned to this task. City libraries are a good source; they have many telephone directories from across the country. You can also find directories in telephone company public offices (where bills are paid).

Besides mailing invitations to former members, consider calling some during low-rate off-hours. Urge friends in the community to invite former members as guests. Encourage families to schedule their own reunions for the same weekend.

Mementos, pictures (especially old and identifiable ones), printed material, individual collections, attics, and members' basements can be drawn upon for the beginning of or additions to a church's historical exhibit. For major anniversaries, writing and publishing a new history is appropriate.

In some celebrations, it is good to have a special series of events during a centennial year, leading up to a climactic Sunday. These can focus on a church's program, with a day or a feature on each of these: (Church name) and Its Ministry to Youth . . . Its Concern for Children . . . and Women's Concerns . . . Its Missionary Outreach . . . Its Daughter Churches (if it has any) . . . Its (mutually supportive relationship to nearby educational or medical institutions).

Or the focus can be on the congregation's support of and concern for meeting major needs in a city. Midweek gatherings might well involve city officials and leaders in stressing the church's relationship and contributions to crime prevention, health care, welfare, schools, good government, and social service.

An anniversary celebration is one of those events in which an entire neighborhood, community, or section of a city should receive direct mail invitations and be given an opportunity to exhibit pictures and items of long-time interest.

Depending on the budget, or whether generous individuals will sponsor specific people of talent, a memorable year can bring to a church, in turn, notables such as a talented author whose roots are in the church, a dance and movement professional who can awaken interests and lead in new directions, a great preacher who would be of interest to a community's national or ethnic constituency differing from that of the celebrating congregation, a popular musician who is at home in a church setting, a recognized authority in Christian education who could help set some goals, or a speaker or writer in church administration to examine resources and point to a new direction.

An anniversary should be a stimulus toward putting a church's property in good order, with repairs, paint, and a general clean-up. It can bring an opportunity to launch a campaign for major additions or new facilities, some of which might be sponsored as individual or family memorials.

If an anniversary does not open new doors for a generous expression of a congregation's missionary concern and outreach, something vital to the church's life and ministry will have been lost. This kind of new commitment to a significant benevolence objective should be at the top of the list, with a definite goal to be reached.

———————•———————

For a wide assortment of possible things to do in an anniversary year, select only as many of the following as you can be sure to do well.

———————•———————

1. Encourage the official board and all major committees to set one or two significant and achievable goals in addition to the usual ones.

2. Design and create new banners, possibly including one or two whose fabric, color, and theme are appropriate for outdoor display.

3. Improve the church's newspaper and/or other advertising.

4. Enlist a group of expert gardeners from the membership to put the church grounds and shrubbery in first-class condition.

5. Begin or update the church's oral history project, recording from the lips of some of the oldest or most interesting members memories of past years. Make this an ongoing project, taking pictures of the individuals at the time of the recording. (Do not fail to get an oral record of any events or experiences that have been more or less traumatic. Even though such recordings might not be used for twenty-five to fifty years, the facts need to be kept in this way.)

6. Find ways to work with local experts in the visual and performing arts, with displays or performances of individual artists during the year.

7. Strengthen ties with other congregations in the neighborhood, in your denominational grouping, and with other denominations and their leaders.

8. Use after-church coffee and social hours for recognition of special individuals and groups.

9. For the year, have a special scrapbook for a complete record. Also maintain a special anniversary year guest book, inserting instant photographs, where possible, alongside signatures.

10. Make a time line around the wall of your largest assembly hall, with pictures inserted at approximate dates. Encourage members to post on this line, and at proper yearly intervals, old bulletins, church or family pictures, wedding announcements, newspaper clippings, birth, baptismal, and wedding certificates (or copies), church school announcements or quarterlies—everything.

11. Bury a time capsule, to be opened in twenty-five or fifty years, containing the widest possible variety of church printed matter and mementos. As space allows, include items from the wider community. Recorded and filmed material should be stored under the guidance of experts to avoid deterioration.

12. Leading up to the anniversary date, publish at regular intervals news items from twenty-five, fifty, seventy-five, and one hundred years earlier.

13. At a nearby shopping mall (or at a fair), have a photograph, slide, or film exhibit featuring aspects of the church's life and activity, with invitations to the celebration.

14. Work with a paper supply house and your own artist to design, develop, and print place mats featuring interesting events in your church's history. These can be used for church affairs, for home meals (if purchased), or in friendly, nearby eating places.

Other Anniversaries

Anniversaries to be noted once in twenty-five, fifty, or one hundred years have been discussed up to this point. There are many others with a more limited scope that are or can be significant.

It is good to have someone in a church who cultivates a detailed knowledge of its history in order to at least mark and make other members aware of different and interesting anniversaries.

Ralph Stoody, long recognized for his effective work in church public relations, encouraged ministers and others to know a congregation's history in detail, recognizing the practical benefits to be gained. He wrote:

> While you are studying the early days, note some beginning dates. When was the first Protestant preaching done in your community? Was it by a minister of your own faith? If not, when was the first sermon preached by a pioneer of your own denomination? When was the first society organized? When was the first church built? When did the present church open for worship? When was the first Sunday school held, the first young people's group instituted, the first woman's society organized? When was the first marriage? Also, when was the first one performed in the present church?
> —from *A Handbook of Church Public Relations*

Not long ago, I saw a church designate a sort of Founders' Day when the members of longer standing were recognized and applauded—for twenty, thirty, forty, or fifty years or more. This need not be an elaborate ceremony, but with special invitations to those members and their family connections, with an after-church reception where certificates or mementos are presented, it can be significant.

Stoody suggests a Family Life Service on the anniversary of the date of the performance of the first marriage ceremony in the church. All of those who have been married in the church or by its pastors, along with descendants of the couple who were first married in the church, would be invited guests of honor for that day. There are several appropriate things to do in this connection, including showing photographs of those weddings and, if possible, tintypes of the first one!

LESSER EVENTS TO CELEBRATE

Many churches have an annual Missions' Day or Week. This can be limited only by local resources and individual imaginations. In today's world, this should never be a routine or traditional observance. Daily headlines are forcing us to deal with issues of hunger, the Third World, the Middle East, Central America, U.S.-Soviet relations, South Africa, and much more.

Some congregations, noted for their vitality and generous support of missions, take an entire week for this emphasis, with worthwhile exhibits and visits and speeches by a succession of missionaries and authorities on the subject. (One Great Hour of Sharing, Worldwide Communion Day, and other generally observed occasions would also profit by an infusion of creative ideas and special emphases.)

Ground-breaking, mortgage-burning, and other traditional events offer opportunities for out-of-the ordinary emphases and, with a little imagination, can be made memorable. I like Stoody's suggestion that a ground-breaking event would be far more significant if, instead of having a few dignitaries do it, we invited all of the church's small children to do one deed with small shovels, like those used at the beach. That would be something for everybody to remember. For mortgage-burning, have a copy of the mortgage shredded; give each person a sliver of the remains to be brought forward during the service and burned in a brazier, or some other fire, while the choir sings a hymn of dedication.

The possibilities for photographs of either event would be more than the usual ones.

THANK YOU, THANK YOU

There may be no better way for a church to demonstrate its grace and graciousness than in the manner in which it expresses appreciation for long or distinguished service. It is sad to see a group of officers, whose terms are expiring, being put aside with minimal expressions, or sometimes none at all.

Faithful teachers of long service, many behind-the-scenes workers such as those who keep the financial records, choir members whose contributions are taken for granted, shut-ins who continue to make noteworthy contributions—these and others need to be identified and in some appropriate way given the church's thanks and evidence of its continuing support.

In the same way, a congregation marked by graciousness will take the initiative in celebrating a pastor's tenure at suitable stages, or even in recognizing twenty-five- or fifty-year anniversaries of the ordination of present or former pastors in situations where that is practical.

Even these modest celebrations need to be planned, with advance announcements in church newsletters and bulletins, a brief focus during morning worship, and a reception after worship. Especially careful thought must always be given in determining who should receive personal invitations, including family, friends, and others who have been associated with the honoree in the area of the distinction being recognized.

PART II
Getting Your Message to the Community

If it is important to use available communications media effectively within the church, it is imperative that it be done in sharing the Christian message with the community. Let's look for a moment at the church's mission and objectives. If we are inclined to think that a church's image or public relations is a matter of indifference or low priority, we don't understand the world in which we live. Public relations is simply an up-to-date term for what has always existed—involving much more, but, in this context, how people think about and how we want them to think about and respond to the church and its efforts.

Has anything brought more revolutionary changes in the last hundred years than what has occurred in the field of communications, including travel? The world has become a neighborhood, at least in geographical terms. We don't have to wait a month, a week, or a day to know what has occurred at the most distant spot on the globe—or even in space. Many of our problems arise from efforts to conduct the church's work and to send forth its message as if this revolution had not occurred.

We need not capitulate to and copy the excesses of the commercial public relations contingent, but we do well to learn what we can and to use what is appropriate for our purposes when the principles are in line with the church's means and motivations. Let us think, in this section, of the image the church has, or we would like it to have, in the eyes of the community.

Your Appearance Says a Lot

BUILDINGS AND GROUNDS

A church building is a constant, round-the-clock witness to what a congregation is and how seriously it takes its mission. Someone aptly said, "A church ought to look as if somebody loves it."

A well-designed building in good repair, set neatly in its pleasant and well-tended grounds, shows that somebody cares and places a premium on the church's mission, or, at least, its image. If it is offering services to individuals in need, and if it has a steady line of people going in and out its doors during the week in a variety of activities, that message is amplified many times. "Beauty is as beauty does." At the least the exterior can be maintained, with the bricks in place, the sidewalks smooth, the trim painted, the windows clean, the steeple and entrance lighted at night, and the bulletin board interesting and up-to-date with frequent changes.

This is not the place for a discussion of church architecture except to say that the church through the ages has, in its better times, been a patron and encourager of the arts. If it aspires to something like that today, the church should not be reluctant to let modern architects and builders do their best with equipment, processes, and materials of our time. Too many buildings are poor copies of architecture and building construction of eras that were not good, certainly not good enough to impose their patterns and practices on our day.

The shape and substance of a church has much to say to everyone who passes it. Its furnishings may tell even more. Set-in-place pews are one common element that actually limit the possibility of drawing people together. Pews often contribute to a performance psychology in church. We expect ministers and musicians to "entertain" us. We need to remember that pews are not "biblical." They are not even traditional over the church's long history. The great cathedrals originally had no pews; people stood in place. Because the cathedral offered the most usable, uncluttered indoor space during the week, it was used for all kinds of community events.

Congregations can be open to this kind of stewardship in our day. A few, but not nearly enough, have movable but substantial seats. What serves as the center for worship on Sunday can be relatively easily converted to a variety of community uses during the week.

Think about the messages a church sends out when it allows its facilities to be used by a variety of congenial community groups. The results of a random survey show something of that variety. The two churches that ranked highest on the survey respectively had eleven and seventeen community or civic groups and agencies meeting within their walls on a scheduled basis. Among the groups gathering at these two churches were: Overeaters Anonymous, Interfaith Council, the Institute of Lifetime Learning, Alcoholics Anonymous, Boy Scouts Council, a social service board, ADAPT (alcohol and drug-related effort), a community college class, three women's clubs and their presidents' council, a Scout leaders' training group, two civic associations, a homemakers club, and a nursing mothers group. Think of what most churches would give if they could attract that kind of traffic and be used in this way. This community involvement says something very powerful to a community in terms of the church's usefulness and willingness to be of service.

Recruit the Green Thumbs

Every church has a few members with green thumbs. They keep their own lawns and grounds in immaculate condition. They know and grow all kinds of beautiful flowers and shrubs. They understand the fundamentals of landscaping or have access to skills in that area.

Invite a few of these experts to form a guild or group to supervise and, perhaps, to work on the church grounds. An hour or two every week or so would pay enormous dividends. A congregation would love and appreciate such a group as it does few others in the church's service. With a ready group to place and plant any shrubs or flowers donated by friends and members, a church yard can be transformed into a place of beauty in a short time.

If churches employ only part-time help for cleaning and maintenance, littered grounds may be a commonplace sight. Littered grounds do not enhance a church's image. Recruit volunteers to police the grounds on a regular schedule, such as during an early morning walk. One environment-conscious churchmember takes a walk early on Sunday mornings (and at other times) around his extended neighborhood, including his own church grounds. At the end of these tours, he has collected a bag full of cans, sticks, papers, and assorted litter, leaving in his wake a cleaner, less cluttered landscape.

Parking Space Provisions

Adequate and convenient parking space can have much to do with whether a church grows or declines. Where the parking lot is located and how it is maintained can be of crucial importance. If it is allowed to grow up in weeds, or if the pavement is broken, or if grass and hedges are not trimmed, or if it is littered with papers and cans, it is speaking to passers-by and the surrounding neighborhood in terms that will do the church no good. Make it someone's daily routine to check the parking areas.

Cultivate the Neighborhood

The goodwill of a church's neighbors is of high importance. When a church building is located or major additions are made, neighbors should be fully informed and, insofar as possible, their ideas and feelings should be respected. It is an unfortunate, and often an unnecessary handicap, for a church to be located in an area where the neighbors harbor ill will against it.

This may be the best place to stress the value of neighborliness on the part of a church and its leaders in other dimensions. It can be of strategic importance to

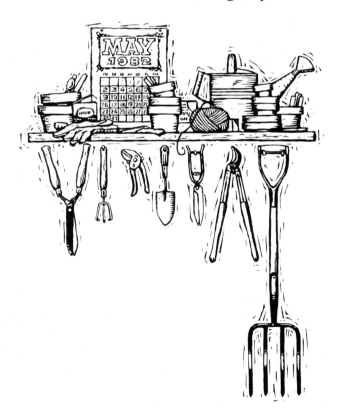

know and be known by the people who operate the most popular nearby gathering places, the service stations, hotels and motels, and the shopping malls. In some of these places it may be appropriate to leave church announcements, schedules, and telephone numbers.

Nearby schools and their leadership should have a priority. Close relationships can make it possible to share colorful and unusual visitors to speak to school groups or assemblies if the ground has been laid. In return, music and drama groups in the schools would appreciate opportunities to perform in the church.

Close and cooperative relationships with the other churches in your community are critical. There is everything to gain and nothing to lose. The pastor can set the tone with genuine, open-handed friendliness and generosity. It is the members, the long-time residents of a community, who can support, encourage, and make cooperation a taken-for-granted practice and tradition. ("The churches in our town always work together!")

In a time of natural disaster, peril, or catastrophic loss by fire or flood, the church and its people are open, instantly available, responsive, and on the scene without calling a meeting to get approval. If ever they are to demonstrate the purpose of their existence and witness to their faith, it should be in such times.

SIGNS AND ANNOUNCEMENT BOARDS

Churches are, or should be, located on or just off major thoroughfares. They are not ordinarily built to be hidden. Spires demand attention. With such exposure, it is very important to have signs of professional quality, giving the name of the church, along the major arteries. This may sometimes be at an intersection. Such signs should be kept clean and well painted because they tell many people something important about the church every day.

Such signs are usually constructed locally by a good painter. Some church supply houses offer an almost all-purpose denominational sign that may be useful in a small town; it may be capable of modification (the addition of a name) for cities with several churches of the same denominational family.

The Outdoor Bulletin Board

Most churches have outdoor boards with glass covers for current announcements of services, special meetings, and the like. Available from church supply houses, they come with an assortment of letters, usually in two or more sizes. A board with good letters will last a lifetime, if it is kept in repair and painted. Such boards should be lighted, with a timer for desired night hours.

Crowding, placing too many words on the board, is a common practice. Most people who see such boards are in passing cars. They may be able to see only a word or two, unless they stop, and they rarely do. For a downtown church, most viewers will be pedestrians who will read more than a few words.

On these boards are usually the ministers' names and the name of the church at the top, the permanent part of the board. In the major space, interchangeable letters announce sermon titles, hours of worship, or up-coming events. (The use of sermon titles is discussed on page 33.)

Such announcements are appropriate for a day or two before the events. For most of the week, churches use striking quotations, usually those that have stood the test of time. Sometimes it may be a Bible verse, but these should be examined carefully to make sure that their words and meaning will be easily understood by those who are not usually in church. Most of the quotations used are "inspirational," giving a lift to the spirits of passers-by, stimulating hope, and offering encouragement in the daily struggle.

It takes time, but it seems to me that concise, current quotations on lively topics chosen from the newspaper or elsewhere would be of more than passing interest. If they are thought-provoking, controversial, or even demagogic, a bottom line could say, "Do you believe that?" or, "What do you think?"

Who is to keep this board fresh, interesting, and up-to-date? That may pose a difficult question. If the minister has time to plan it, he or she is offered a rather special opportunity to preach in a few well-chosen words. If a few members of exceptional alertness and perception are willing to participate in the ministry, all the better.

Leaving signs unchanged, with the same words week after week, makes a poor impression on those who pass by. Where an announcement board is the bearer of good news, inspiring phrases, provocative inquiries, and reminders of our heritage, all who come by it can be reasonably sure that something interesting and important is taking place.

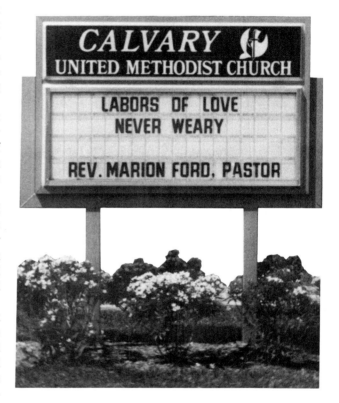

Outdoor Banners

For special events, or as permanent features, it is possible to make or have made all-weather banners to add a touch of color and distinction to the church grounds. In considering the cost for long-time use, be sure to take special care in selecting the design and color. Mounted on a pipe framework and secured at both ends but not stretched tight, banners can last for some years through wind and weather.

Making Friends with the Public Media

THE LOCAL NEWSPAPER

It was a great and memorable Sunday at St. Maximus Church. The denominational president was there for a visit and to preach. The church was neat, with everything in order. The choirs were never better. Every seat was filled. When, if ever, had any church event worked out so well?

The next morning, when the pastor and members turned to their local paper, there was nothing there, not a line. "After all," members said, "that paper is interested only in controversy. If we had been having a fight in the congregation, it would have been spread all over the front page."

At Third Middleground Church, the story was different. Before a similar event, the Saturday paper carried an attention-getting picture of the visiting official, with an extended and friendly interview about the national denomination and how chuches like Third Middleground were meeting their opportunities. On Monday morning, there was a picture and an account of the service, with a couple of good quotations from the sermon.

What made the difference? There are several possible explanations.

No one at St. Maximus talked ahead of time (at least two weeks) with the religion editor or reporter. Instead, a comprehensive packet of advance information was dropped off at the newspaper office on the preceding Saturday morning, too late to be of any use; or carbon copies of a general news story were mailed to the editor; or, perhaps, the head of the event's planning committee thought someone else was taking care of the job.

Third Middleground prepared well. The pastor, who had made himelf known to the religion editor as friendly and cooperative, had been a source of news items before, and not simply about Third Middleground. Several weeks before the scheduled event, he telephoned the editor to brief her on the plans, saying something like this: "I don't know what else will be claiming your attention that weekend, but if we can be of any help in getting what you want from us—like an interview before the date or anything else—you know that you have only to ask me. We have pictures, but if you want to arrange for your own, we will work with you."

In addition, a well-prepared background story was written and sent to the religion editor a week in advance, with a penned note saying, "This is background information on the event we talked about. Please call me if you need anything else. If you want to do the interview by telephone before our speaker arrives, here's the number to call. . . . "

On Sunday morning, a church officer was stationed at a lookout point for the editor, to welcome her and to show her to a good seat, to introduce her to the speaker and, if desired, to arrange for a few minutes of follow-up questions.

In some cases, the prepared text of the sermon or address can be in hand to give to the reporter or editor ahead of time, if the sermon is coming to grips with current or lively issues.

While it is easy to blame the newspaper when we fail to get the coverage we think we deserve, the fault may very well be, and often is, found in the church's inadequate preparation or failure to establish fruitful contacts. I once heard an Associated Press bureau chief say, "When you take a news item to the local paper, don't go in saying, 'Here's something we want you to print for us,' or, 'We hope you can give us some publicity on this coming event.' Instead, you should tell briefly what is coming up and ask, 'What can we do to help you get the story you want out of this?' It is always, *what can we do to help you?*"

The newspaper owes us nothing as news providers. It is (or should be) interested only in doing the best possible job in getting the news to its readers. It is to our distinct advantage to help the newspapers do their job well.

News interest and values are important, but personal contacts are basic. A news item coming from someone who is known personally (and favorably) takes on an added value or importance.

A new pastor, friendly and outgoing toward everybody, came to town. He knew very well what he was doing when he had one of his knowledgeable members take him to the newspaper offices and introduce him to the religion editor and other reporters. That was not all. They went also to the advertising department to become acquainted with those who would be handling the weekly church advertisement. Something like this is easy to do, and the benefits can be far-reaching. Similar contacts by church members responsible for press relationships are just as important.

A media director has high praise for an on-the-ball civic/political organization whose contact person is changed every year or two. When the change is made, there is an immediate visit, call, or letter telling about the change. The new person introduces himself or herself, and lists telephone numbers and an offer to provide any needed information. That makes a good impression and pays dividends.

What Can We Do to Help You?
10 Tips for Working with Your Local Newspaper

1. Establish and nourish personal contacts.
2. Don't overload the editor with routine announcements.
3. Submit only what is *news*—or of special interest.
4. Offer a complete information packet at least two weeks before a major event.
5. Provide good pictures or help in arrangements for the newspaper's photographer.
6. Submit news releases or stories typed double-spaced on one side of 8" x 11" white paper with name, address, and phone number in the upper left corner.
7. Always cover *who, what, when, where,* and if appropriate, *why* and *how,* in your stories and information.
8. Know and respect newspaper deadlines.
9. Let your attitude always be: "What can we do to help you?"
10. Give generous praise for good coverage.

What Is News?

There may be no greater confusion in church offices than in failing to distinguish between announcements and news. Newspapers have little interest in announcements except in their advertising columns and, perhaps, in a Saturday column on the "religion" page, devoted to brief public service notices. Let us look first at those notices.

Newspapers are willing, sometimes glad, to carry such announcements without charge, but they must be short, cleanly and accurately typed, and in hand before the stated deadline—usually about three days before publication. They will not be accepted by telephone.

Care should be taken not to abuse the privilege of having announcements appear in the news columns. That is, send one in only occasionally—when you have planned something out of the ordinary—and not to list a usual Sunday service and sermon. For small-town newspapers, other practices may prevail.

These notices should not be crowded on a typed page. Use double- or triple-spacing. The name and telephone number of the person submitting the notice must appear in the upper lefthand corner. Sometimes if the possibility of a news story or picture might result from the scheduled event, a brief note at the bottom of the sheet (and away from the notice) might suggest your willingness to supply or help provide one or both if desired. If someone's name appears in the notice (like a special speaker) there is nothing to lose and much to be gained if his or her telephone number is shown on the lower part of the page, separate from the announcement.

One imperative in such notices, as in news stories is that you make certain that nothing is misspelled, that all references and dates are correct, and that full names and initials are used. A poorly written announcement, punctuated by careless errors, will be promptly dropped into the wastebasket, and with it, the credibility of the person or institution submitting it.

News stories are what editors are most interested in receiving, not bulletin anouncements. Editors want news of general interest. You can test the newsworthiness of your announcement by asking whether you would be interested in reading it if it told about something in another church. If it is unique, unusual, or off-beat, and most of all, controversial, its value will be greater. (In my judgment, some papers put so much emphasis on the controversial that they often blind themselves to the interest and excitement in news stories about creative, innovative, and constructive enterprises in churches. But you can't overcome editorial attitudes about this. Don't try persuasion. You can only hope to find a reporter or editor who has a broader sense of news value and what people are interested in reading.)

Submitted news stories have a much greater chance of being used (even though they may be rewritten) if standard procedures are followed. That is, type the story double- or triple-spaced on one side of white paper, beginning about four inches from the top of the sheet. In the upper left corner, put your name, address, and telephone number. On the upper right side, and only if delay is imperative, write: "For Release on (date)" (but never use a release date for broadcast media. What they receive is for today!).

At the bottom of the first page, if there is to be a second page, write **MORE.** At the end of the story, write # # # or 30. (Thirty is not used nearly so often by the professionals as it is by the amateurs.)

Look in your newspaper for a relatively brief news story. Study it. See how it is constructed—like a pyramid, with the most important information at the top and less important material and more details as it continues. This is not only because it is a logical and interesting way to write it, but also because written in this way, it can be cut off beginning with the last paragraph and moving up, as needed, without losing the most important facts. Newspaper columns are only so long, and news stories must be cut to fit.

Six Serving Men

How do you determine what is important? Rudyard Kipling, in his *Just So Stories,* a long time ago gave us some helpful lines summarizing the five W's and the H:

> I keep six honest serving-men
>   (They taught me all I knew);
> Their names are What and Why and When
>   And How and Where and Who.
>   —from *The Elephant's Child*

You must determine which of these is most important for your particular story and lead-off with it in a well-focused, fairly short opening sentence. It will be more easily read if you can start a new paragraph next, with simple, straightforward sentences, giving the rest of the essentials. Use action-packed verbs and few adjectives. Avoid long sentences and paragraphs. Paragraphs with much more than thirty-five words don't read well.

The first sentence in the Bible, "In the beginning, God created the heavens and the earth," is often used as a perfect illustration of how to give the essentials—all of the W's are present except the Why. While the W's and the H have long been considered almost inviolable, it is possible to have a good story if you don't follow that formula, so long as you provide the essentials. You can check to see how your completed story will read if the editor cuts off the last paragraph, then the next, and the next. Just be sure that what is left contains what, in your judgment, is most important.

Often the best attention is focused on a picture, with the essential information in a few lines (called "cut lines") beneath it. A telephone suggestion or inquiry about possible interest to a reporter or editor may result in having a newspaper photographer sent to take a picture. If you learn to see picture possibilities, you can reap many benefits. (Remember that newspapers want black and white pictures only.)

In meeting their responsibilities, reporters routinely check with area denominational offices. They make it their business to keep in touch with top officials. With something very important, you might do well to tell the officials of your denomination about a news or picture idea that could be passed along to the newspaper.

Learned by Experience

Now for assorted suggestions:

- Know the newspaper deadlines and respect them. Have your story in well ahead of time. A follow-up call, offering additional help, is appropriate provided it is not at or near press time, is not lengthy, and is not made often.

- Do not over-expose the pastor by making him or her always the source of comments or information from your church. Also quote members and leaders who are heading up the enterprise being reported.

- If your church becomes involved in a publicized controversy, don't try to hide or deny it. It will all come out in the long-run, and it is better for responsible leaders to provide accurate information at the beginning. You will make friends and create confidence with the reporters, the editors, and the public by doing so.

- Be timely. Let the newspaper know about major steps that are being planned, as with full information about where a departing minister is going and all about a new one coming. The latter can usually be done just before a decision is to be made so that full details (and a picture) are in hand for the next day's paper. Editors like that.

- Invite religion reporters and editors (every few years or soon after a change) to meet with pastors and church representatives to discuss ways in which the churches can help get the news they want and can use. This may be done on a community basis better than in a single church or denomination.

- Many religion reporters and editors keep up-to-date files on the major (usually controversial) church-related issues being discussed across the nation. Since they often see the action close-up at regional and national meetings, they would be glad to accept invitations to church groups and classes to tell what is going on. Beyond the information gained, this is a good way to establish valuable ties with the newspapers.

- Once more, remember to use clear, simple words and constructions in what you write, no long and complicated sentences, no theological jargon.

- Be quick to praise—to express appreciation—for whatever you consider to have been done well. Doesn't the adage say, "Honey catches more flies than vinegar"?

Is It Possible?

I have long cherished what may be a forlorn hope.

Every Saturday, the metropolitan papers, more than seventeen hundred dailies in this country, have their pages of church notices and advertising, telling about the high promise of what will be happening the next day. The more than sixty-seven hundred weeklies in the smaller towns and communities have already added their part to the atmosphere of expectation.

But do you ever . . . ever . . . see anything in Monday's paper about what was scheduled, anything of news value or interest in the thousands of sermons preached?

I know. Preachers are not tuned, and had better not be tuned, to the newspaper's expectations. They are preaching for more ultimate judgments. But I would like, at least occasionally, to see something said in terms of Christian good news or witness in regard to a crucial public issue that is given news prominence.

I believe that much is being preached that would qualify. I believe that if two or three brief paragraphs on lively issues were given to the editor ahead of time, a news story would appear in Monday's paper. Those quotations would have to be sharp and unequivocal. I believe they would be printed and would be useful.

I keep hoping.

ADVERTISING THE CHURCH

While there are recognized limits of taste and propriety in church advertising, there are persuasive arguments for it within those bounds. It has been claimed that the first advertisement, probably on a sheet of parchment, appeared before 3,000 B.C., offering a reward for a runaway slave. One church advertising advocate puts it this way: "People have run away from their Creator, and church advertising should be designed and used to get them back."

I know of no church that would object to being featured in a newspaper story. Objections to church advertising seem to come chiefly from having to pay for the space.

In smaller towns, the only paid church advertising is often that provided by one or more commercial establishments, with the names of churches, ministers, and hours of services listed compactly in small type. I have my doubts as to the value of this to anyone except the newspaper. There it may be considered a degree of compensation for church items carried elsewhere in the paper, usually a great many of them.

In cities, paid notices, one or two inches in depth, are usually grouped by denomination on a Saturday church or religion page, often with a listing of the sermon topic and the preacher's name. I have expressed my reservations about sermon topics elsewhere (page 9). I am not convinced of the effectiveness of these small ads.

It would seem to me to be better, at least worth the experiment, for a church to take an occasional space of at least four or five column inches on another page and designed on an entirely different pattern. The article must be carefully thought out, well designed, and have especially chosen (and tested?) wording like some of the examples given below. A free brochure could be offered, dealing with a lively issue being discussed at the time or something concerned with personal and inner growth, such as: "How to Read the Bible with Understanding" or "How to Develop an Effective Prayer Life." I believe there would be a grateful response to such offers.

Where the churches in a community will pool their advertising budgets, those in the same denomination can make effective joint presentations; they can make the kind of evangelistic appeal to the "runaway slaves" that all could support. Or they could deal with the deeper meanings of Christmas, Easter, Thanksgiving, and so on. In these types of articles, churches might do no more for their own identification than to list their names, addresses, telephone numbers, and the names of their ministers.

In place of the Saturday listings of Sunday schedules and sermons, again, if cross-denominational groups of churches pooled their advertising money, they could follow at least one or two courses. They could plan a well-designed advertisement, with suitable art work and eye-catching appeal, which would provide a listing of their respective churches with addresses and names of their ministers. If there are many churches, it would be better to do this in turn by areas of a city, featuring a section of the city map and showing the location of each church on the map. Again, this might be placed on other than the church page.

Some denominational national offices have kits of material to help churches wrestle with this problem. Some of them have readily available advertisements that can be used or adapted to local use. It would seem that these churches have had the benefit of the judgment of experts in the field, both in wording and in design. Some, obviously, are better than others. Each of these is in the context of appropriate illustrations:

(1)

(2)

Office of Communications, American Lutheran Church, 422 S. Fifth, Minneapolis, Minn. 55415
The United Methodist Church. United Methodist Communications, 810 12th Ave. S., Nashville, Tenn. 37203
Available from The Advertising Council, Inc., 825 Third Avenue, New York, NY 10022

Religion in American Life (RIAL) has, for a good many years, developed and made available to newspapers an annual series of advertisements that are not only acceptable to members of all faiths, but also serve as models of good advertising with a wide appeal, which should be studied by those interested in creating their own.

Communications headquarters of national church bodies, like those listed here [(1), (2), (3)] not only give specific help in fashioning good advertising, but they also provide, at modest cost, a variety of informative pamphlets and reprints of broadcast and cable television programs, church newsletters, telephone skills, video evangelism, church and newspaper relations, and so forth.

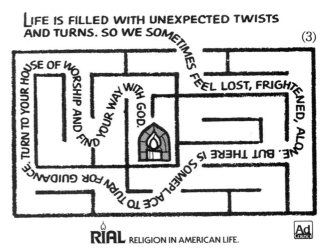

(3)

RELIGION IN AMERICAN LIFE CAMPAIGN
NEWSPAPER AD NO. RIAL-85-912—2 COL.

In Smaller Communities

While situations differ, my observation and experience tell me that the weekly papers offer a special opportunity for the church, especially for anyone who understands or has any skill or experience in journalism or public relations. Personal and friendly relations are normal and easy to cultivate.

News stories written in reasonably good newspaper style are welcomed. A devotional bit that might be an excerpt from a sermon might even become a regular and appreciated feature. Also, a column of brief miscellaneous paragraphs of comment and quotation would brighten many a newspaper if no remuneration is expected. Also, letter-type reports from travel abroad or from unusual events in this country might be welcomed if arranged ahead of time.

Any church or pastor gaining such a privileged opportunity would do well to handle it carefully, with full and gracious attention to churches other than one's own.

One church made interesting use of classified ads to draw the attention of its community to a sermon series on "Stories of the Beginning," dealing with well-known biblical characters. Two of the ads read:

DID ADAM get back into the Garden of Eden? Come to hear the story at the _____ Church, Sunday at 11:00 A.M..

YOU THINK you are a businessman? Learn something from Jacob next Sunday at the _____ Church at 11:00 A.M.

Another idea is to piggyback on big-space advertising of stores owned or operated by one's own members, with two or three lines highlighting a special event in a small set-apart corner or space in the larger ad.

Other Advertising

The usual costs of billboard displays make this medium impractical for most church considerations, but there are ways. Only for a mighty, united citywide effort would it seem at all likely that billboards would be used, even with advertisers' assurances that you will attract the attention of more of the young, the affluent, the educated, the professional, and the managerial groups than of the population as a whole. Despite the fact that you will do this more often (85.3 percent of the adults in an average market on an average of 24.7 times each in a month), this is not a thirty-second spot that flashes and is gone; it lasts for a month. Furthermore, a billboard measures from 200 square feet to more than 600 square feet in some cases.

If you cannot afford the cost, here are some possibilities:

Billboard companies are eager to cooperate on a public service basis, giving the space for a united cause or emphasis. All you have to do is plan and pay the cost of the printed sheets or posters. This might even be done for a united church message or emphasis in mid-winter, the slow season. One such eye-catching billboard had this message:

C H   C H
What's missing?

Preparation of some printed sheets can run from less than $100 to $1,500 or more. The cost of renting billboards is substantial, depending on the number used and the area served.

Some big businesses have their own billboards on their own property. Sometimes they permit them to be used for church or public service messages.

Where a church owns an unused lot on a heavily traveled street, investigate the possibility of erecting a billboard for church use.

Mobile billboards can be rented for special greetings or to herald special events.

Although newspaper advertising is, doubtless, the most traditional and easily available medium, it may not be the most effective. We are habituated to think that print is the primary, if not the only, medium available to us, but most people are being stimulated and influenced more by audio-visuals than by what they read in print. Cable television is opening up opportunities. Specialists at national church headquarters should be consulted about ways to use this medium. Although some national media offices offer tested television spots for local use, the cost is usually more than a church is willing to spend, or more than it should spend.

Radio reaches many people, especially those in cars, and costs are not excessive. But available money can be easily wasted if some specific questions are not worked through, such as: What are you seeking to accomplish? Who is the target audience (age, special interests, education)? And which of the local stations is reaching enough of that target audience to justify the expenditure? (Direct mail may often be a better course to follow.)

THE BROADCAST MEDIA

Relatively few churches will be in a position to have their services or any other feature carried on television. A few, usually patterning their programs on the style of the highly publicized preachers, do so, but few will even try to justify the cost or regard this as the appropriate image they should seek to project. Use of cable television for teaching and the discussion of significant issues is another matter.

We are only beginning to see the possibilities open to us on the cables. Public access channels are available and are mostly unused, but few churches are equipped with the skills required to take advantage of them. So far, videotapes prepared by experts are the best hope, though church leaders will do well to examine carefully any that may be bought or rented for this use. If not, we may easily broadcast interpretations of the faith and images of the church that we will regret. (Every major denomination has an abundance of information, with guidelines, available on request, or for a small charge.)

Radio is still used by many churches to broadcast their major services at a modest cost. This is done either live or on a delayed basis. While the experts have long contended that this is a waste of time and effort, with car radios everywhere, in addition to individuals whose interest is stimulated by word-of-mouth comments, there are measurable results. A church can do a great deal to impress a community with its friendly spirit, its broadening concerns, and its responsiveness. (It is always better if the sermons are good.)

Public service announcements (PSAs) on television and radio are required of each station. One media director exclaims: "What churches can get free of charge is unbelievable!" However, stations are not required to use everything sent to them. The volume is too great, but they do their best. Some stations will not use "bake sale" and similar notices. Guidelines from radio stations:

Public Service Announcements

- Keep them short.
- Make them accurate.
- Give full information.
- Don't engulf us with a flood of paper.
- Be selective.
- Don't send them too often.
- Give a name and telephone number for further information or corroboration.

To gain credibility and attention, type accurately and neatly, spell correctly, and be sure of names, times, and addresses. Double or triple space.

Broadcast News

If it is important with public service announcements, it is even more important in getting attention for broadcast news that you have a personal contact. As one media expert put it, "Let them see *you* rather than always just a piece of paper."

Just as you need to know and keep in touch with editors and reporters, you need to know the broadcast people. Use their names in what you send to the stations. Keep up (and, if possible, maintain personal ties) with directors, managers, and reporters. Don't address anything to someone who is no longer employed at the station. These personal contacts will not guarantee the kind of coverage you would like to have, but they don't hurt.

As with newspapers, you dare not demand, or even request, publicity or coverage. You will do well to inquire as to what you can do to help the broadcaster get the story. Also, to make sure that you have something of genuine news value, test its possible interest to you if it were about another church or event.

Know and follow the station deadlines. Radio news deadlines are usually every hour, but the news director will tell you specifically about the major deadlines. For television news, 3:00 P.M. is usually the deadline for the six o'clock news, and a comparable advance time for ten or the eleven o'clock news. You can learn specifics from the news room.

Interviews of special speakers or leaders are at a premium. In arranging for interviews, personal contacts can be of major importance.

Separate news releases for radio and television, different from what goes to the newspapers, are recommended. Make them concise, but with full information—the five W's: who, what, when, where, why. And never say, "For release (at a later date)." What they get, they use now.

Remember that these are *people* who are doing the job. They deserve and appreciate words of praise and gratitude as much as anybody.

Religion is regarded and treated as a touchy, sensitive subject by many radio and television people. Experts who work with them believe that this is caused largely by the electronic preachers who have left a bad taste in the mouth of many. Broadcasters have come to regard religion as news only if it is controversial. They think that there may be many booby-traps out there. They walk cautiously or keep away altogether from what they think is a mined field. This is another reason for the church's leaders to make warm, friendly, and continuing contacts.

Using Direct Mail and Other Printed Pieces

Next to a ready-to-use telephone network, direct mail is the quickest means of communication available to a church, both within the congregation and in the community. With the mailing of newsletters, campaign appeals, solicitations for special or emergency gifts, along with the annual stewardship emphasis, direct mail is the most used method of getting publicity.

Although third-class postal rates are higher than ever, they still offer the most economical means of putting important information in the hands of members or non-members. Churches and other non-profit organizations receive a special per-piece rate. For this, specific guidelines have to be followed in preparing the envelopes or other pieces for mailing. These guidelines are available from the post office. (There must be at least two hundred identical pieces in one mailing!)

First-class letters are also "direct mail," and it has been thought by many that any letter of importance must be sent at the full rate. I cannot think of a mailing to a congregation that would justify first-class postage, unless the total is well below the two hundred minimum.

In most post offices, third-class mailings are processed promptly, with local delivery usually the next day.

LETTERS

We receive so many third-class letters in what we call "junk mail" that most of us should be able to recognize what makes a good letter, one that catches our attention and leads to a favorable response. If the sheet is crowded, poorly typed or printed, with long sentences and paragraphs, we may not even try to read it. That may also be true if the envelope is gaudy and the type comes shouting out at us.

If the margins are good, if the type is easy to read, and the sentences are reasonably short, we are more likely to read the letter. But even within those specifications,

---

How to Write a Letter . . . That Will be Read!

1. Think of your audience—your readers.
2. Spend time developing a first sentence that grabs the reader.
3. Use wide margins and put extra space between paragraphs.
4. Write short paragraphs.
5. Use underlining and, if possible, color for emphasis.
6. Be sure type is clear and clean, easy to read.
7. Check and *recheck* for errors in spelling and grammar.
8. End your letter with a well-focused thought or appeal.
9. Consider a short one- or two-line message on the envelope.
10. *Test* your letter on a small group and *listen* to the responses.

much depends on what is said and how it is worded. An expert in this field once said, "Your first ten words are more important than your next ten thousand." A good beginning is worth many trials and tests. Write it in all kinds of ways, but test it out until you find the best one. This will involve not beginning with something about yourself or what you think; it will begin with something that is almost certain to interest the reader. Think how it will seem and how it will be read by those who receive it.

Reading is made easier by white space, indented paragraphs, underlined words, a spot of color if possible, a one-sentence paragraph and that a short one. Ordinarily, one page is enough, though longer letters about exciting, crucial, or emergency situations will be read. It still helps to keep the pages easy to read.

A good closing paragraph or sentence is important. Rewriting several times will pay dividends.

Check carefully and have someone else double-check for spelling and grammatical slips and errors of fact. You don't want these to divert attention.

If you can make a small test—even with six to ten people—do so. Their honest reactions will help you.

A well thought out line printed on the envelope, if it is a good one, may stimulate interest and increase the likelihood that the letter will be opened.

POST CARDS

Cards can be sent first class at eight cents less than a letter. They are very effective communication tools that I have used often and with success.

The cards may be about the size of government postal cards or any of several other sizes. To be processed by the post office, they must be at least 5 inches long, 3½ inches high, and at least the thickness of a government postal card. They cannot exceed 6⅛ inches in height, 11½ inches in length, and 1/4 inch in thickness. They cannot have a length less than 1⅓ times the height or more than 2½ times the height.

Printed cards of different sizes are used well, sometimes with good, eye-catching art, sometimes typed creatively, always with a sharply-focused message. They can be used to build attendance, take a poll, create interest in an enterprise, furnish brief or emergency directions quickly, gather information and much more.

Colored stock, if it is not dark, with bold, contrasting ink is effective. Many colors are available from paper supply houses.

COVER THE COMMUNITY

At least once every year or so churches do well to make a carefully-planned mass mailing—to every house within, say, a half-mile of their locations. Or, it could be within a well-defined area or postal zone. Compile a mailing list to RESIDENT at each listed address. The mailing list can be purchased (check your yellow pages). In small towns, every home can be included.

In such mailings, special care must be taken to insure against an impression of attempting to steal sheep from neighboring flocks, but this can be done in terms of sharing facilities or special features with the community-at-large. This could be a recreational opportunity, a vacation Bible school, a musical event, a dedication, anniversary or a seasonal or special celebration. Whatever the event or program, the message should be a bountiful, open-handed gesture of generosity and goodwill, with more concern for giving than for getting.

A mailing of this character could take the form of an earnest inquiry, asking, "What urgent need of our area (or community) would you like to see the churches (or, this church) meeting better than they are now doing? Send in your suggestions (spell out details), or come to talk it over (date and place of meeting) to help us have a better neighborhood (or community)."

A church's mass mailing to its neighborhood could give details about an outdoor Christmas display, or about a new bell or tower chimes (with requests for reactions).

DIRECT MAIL CASE STUDY

An illustration may help to emphasize the importance of direct mail in helping to reach an objective common to all churches. The objective is motivating members to respond to and participate in an event that will be rewarding to them and to the entire church.

The course too often followed runs like this: General announcements will be made, over and over, calling on "everybody" to take advantage of the opportunity; sometimes, for "anybody" who can find time for it. These announcements are made from the pulpit, in all church gatherings, in the newsletter, and in the bulletin. Brochures are placed on a hall table where "anyone" may happen to pick one up; they are also posted on the bulletin board. If effective communication is tested by response, no communication is taking place.

There are better ways. The event portrayed as a case in point is the annual Leadership Fair for all churches of the denomination in one city. Sixteen courses or workshops are offered on a Sunday afternoon, led by topflight teachers, some brought in from a distance. The offerings are first-class, with far-reaching benefits awaiting each participant and, in turn, every church whose members are present.

The pastor or church educator sits down with three or four leaders who know the congregation and who are aware of the church's teacher/leadership needs. They look at the course offerings, and run through the list of members, matching up prospective participants with courses. They may set a goal of 10 or 15 percent of the membership, or even more.

The list is presented to the appropriate administrative committee or the church's official board, with a request for support and endorsement in recruiting the prospective participants. With that support, a personal letter like the one following is written to each one:

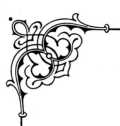

Dear ——————,

    As we move into the fall program of our church, your valuable contribution to our work makes me thank God for you and for your sustained and ready witness. Your cheerful response and your influence in our congregation are big assets as we try to measure up to our opportunities.

    You know how we are always trying to encourage our members to take advantage of special opportunities that come our way. I am writing you about one of these.

    Our Official Board has designated you to be invited to participate in our citywide cooperative Leadership Faire (at——————) on Sunday afternoon, September 28.

    Because of your responsibilities and demonstrated skills, I want to suggest that you consider enrolling for Course No. 2 on "Teaching Children," which will be taught by Sarah Griggs, whose reputation in this field makes her an authority. For you to take advantage of this offering will make a direct contribution to our program, but if you have a more compelling interest in another course, please feel free to enroll for it.

    By the way, if (spouse) can possibly arrange it, I want to suggest Course No. 8 on "Peacemaking," taught by Randy Payne, who is one of the best.

    Our church will pay the registration fee for this, but your enrollment form should be sent in at once. On the enclosed brochure on which I have written your name, I have checked the suggested course. You will find full details in it.

    Please know of my gratitude for your always dependable cooperation and my prayers for you and yours,

        Your friend and pastor,

            (signed) ——————
            (typed) ——————

    P.S. I expect to be with you on September 28 because I have signed up for Course no. 12 on "Recruiting and Motivating Leaders in the Church's Educational Program."

This will be effective, but it is not all.

In addition to full publicity in the newsletter, the bulletin, and elsewhere, preview presentations by committee leaders or planners, there will be one-to-one follow-up in conversation or by telephone by designated individuals. Those who sign up will be recognized and commended in an appropriate manner. On the day of the event, they will be remembered with gratitude in the morning prayer. They will be mentioned in suitable gatherings in the church and, if at all possible, sent thank-you letters afterward.

Pastors and leaders will show in all suitable ways how important they consider a major event like this, and participation in it, to be. Church members don't always do what pastors think is important, but they will scarcely, if ever, do what a pastor seems to think is unimportant.

People can be counted on to respond to significant challenges and invitations if the opportunity is dignified by being made personal instead of general, and if it is shown to be important. It is surprising to discover how many members have never been personally asked to represent their church or to do something significant in its name. They have heard innumerable general appeals, but none in which they were singled out by name.

OTHER PRINTED PIECES

From the longer list of folders, booklets, cards, brochures, and other kinds of printed pieces, let me comment on two: folders and brochures. Cards have already been discussed under direct mail.

Folders

The best bargain in this category, and one of the easiest to prepare and mail, is what I am calling a folder, usually an 8½-by-11-inch sheet, printed on one or both sides. It can be folded in half, with half of one side for the postal indicia, address and return information. Since this must meet postal specifications, be sure to check it out with the post office.

The sheet can be folded twice, providing three sections of almost 3¾", one of which can be used for address, postal entry number, etc., leaving two-thirds of that side for a continuation of page one.

Such a sheet can be an adaptation of old-time broadsides, featuring a coming event, with art and drawings to suit. A good many church newsletters take this form. As many pages as may be desired can be stapled and sent in this form.

Folders are utilitarian, not usually prepared for looks and style, but it helps to remember that every mailing contributes its part to the image recipients have of the church.

Brochures

Brochures are usually thought of as having a longer-lasting quality than a folder. This format is useful in describing or providing information about special or continuing programs. They are usually four pages or multiples of four in a wide variety of sizes. They are usually commercially printed, with appropriate art and layout, with good, readable type on good paper, and in ink that is dark and in bold contrast to the paper. A glossy, slick-finish paper does not provide the best reading surface. The color of the paper or ink should not make the text hard to read. (Color is better for accents and emphasis.)

Brochures can be prepared for distribution to prospective or non-members, describing the life and work of the church. They can delineate a comprehensive music program and opportunities to participate in it. They can detail the extensive Christian education program and its leadership. They can tell dramatically and with pictures, something of a church's far-flung missionary-support projects. They can focus on cherished traditions and what they mean, or an interpretation of a church's symbols and those common to Christian history. Possibilities are endless.

Denominational supply houses have many kinds of brochures, usually emphasizing some of their distinctive tenets or traditions, but nearly always with some that would be useful in other churches.

While a few brochures or leaflets may be placed in a narthex rack to be taken by those who are interested, this is not the most effective distribution method. It is far better to send them, preferably with a brief note or handwritten message, to those who might be most interested in them, or to provide them to members to place in the hands of such individuals. They may be left on a home visit or offered in a church advertisement to be sent free upon request. They may sometimes be placed in the pews for a specific use, but not left there indefinitely.

A CASE STUDY: MAKING IT ALL WORK

The annual community-wide leadership event was being planned for an approaching Sunday afternoon. It was for teachers, church officers, and congregational leaders, but some offerings were always designated for "ordinary" members. Many kinds of promotion were used, including a well-designed and printed brochure, personal recruiting in the churches, and an advance dinner for key people to inspire and encourage participants in their own efforts and to share the mounting enthusiasm.

Frank, who had long maintained good working relationships with the media people, was in charge of press, radio, and television coverage. About a month before the big day, he gave a brief narrative on the coming event to his reporter-contact, describing what it was all about and indicating its importance.

One course was to be offered for those with responsibility for preparing and serving church dinners. He had a picture of the teacher in a chef's apron. This he gave, not to the religion editor or his primary reporter-contact, but to the editor of the food section where it received big attention with an accompanying story.

For different uses in morning and afternoon papers, he thought of picture possibilities and suggested them, putting a spotlight on one or more specific offerings instead of the entire program, or giving priority to a special out-of-town teacher of considerable note. He let the papers know what was available on particular courses and teachers.

He worked with his TV contact for a good interview about the school on the leading television station.

The results of all of this were predictable, with high, if not record-breaking, attendance.

Frank is sure that you must let the media know what you have for their possible use, you must help them get more if needed, and you must work to suit their time and convenience. You must also praise and thank the reporters and broadcasters who cooperated. Finally, he says, keep your contacts alive. There may be other days when you will need them and will be glad for them.

"The king's business required haste" (I Samuel 21:8) has often been transposed to suggest that God's work claims the top priority; let nothing push it aside. No emphasis has been more important in these pages than the fact that communicating the church's message and sharing the life of our community of faith have a right to a first claim on our energies. Offering our best in this as in all other areas of the work of the kingdom brings enduring satisfactions.

Some Helpful
Books and Sources

General

Austin, Charles M. *Let the People Know*. Minneapolis, MN: Augsburg, 1975.

Craig, Floyd A. *A Christian Communicator's Handbook*. Nashville: Broadman, 1977.

DeVries, Charles, editor. (Written by public relation professionals.) *Religious Public Relations Handbook*. New York: Religious Public Relations Council, 1982.

Jackson, B.F. *You and Communication in the Church: Skills and Techniques*. Waco, TX: Word, 1974.

Swann, Charles E., *The Communicating Church*. Atlanta, GA: Media Communications, Presbyterian Church, 1981.

Writing

Flesch, Rudolph. *The Art of Readable Writing*. New York: MacMillan, 1962.

Fairfax, John and Moat, John. *The Way to Write*. New York: St. Martin, 1982.

Strunk, William and White, E. B. *The Elements of Style*. New York: Macmillan, 1979.

Newsletters

How-To News: a Manual on Church Newsletter. New York: Gotwals, Martha and Schneider, Eugene, eds. United Church of Christ Office of Communication, 1983. (105 Madison Ave. New York, NY 10016)

Advertising

Dunkin, Steve. *Church Advertising: A Practical Guide*. Nashville: Abingdon Press, 1982.

Telephone

Dowdy, Augustus W. Jr. *Phone Power*. Valley Forge, Penn.: Judson, 1975.

Schneider, Eugene A. *How-To Telephone*, a manual on the use of the telephone by the church. New York: United Church of Christ Office of Communication, 1977.

Bulletin Boards and Banners

Brannon, Robert, *The Banner Book*. Nashville: Abingdon Press, 1986.

McCartney, Carol. *The Great Bulletin Board Idea Book, Vols. 6 I* and *II*. Nashville: Abingdon Press, 1986.

Photographs

For a variety of instructional pamphlets and books, contact the Eastman Kodak Company, Rochester, NY 14650.

Clip Art

The Great Clip Art Book For All Occasions. Nashville: Abingdon Press, 1986.

For *clip art* also contact: Dynamic Graphics, Inc.; 6707 N. Sheridan Road, Peoria, IL 61614; and Volk Corporation, 1401 N. Main Street, Pleasantville, NJ 06232

Direct Mail

Direct mail newsleter available from Boise Cascade Envelope Division, 313 Rohlwing Road (Rt. 53), Addison, IL 60101